IT'S YOUR TIME TO SHINE!

**WEEKLY SPIRITUAL
REFLECTIONS FOR WOMEN**

Nicole Roberts Jones

THE PILGRIM PRESS
CLEVELAND

IT is with great admiration and gratitude that I dedicate this book to my pastor and spiritual father, Dr. Cecil L. "Chip" Murray. You believed in me when I was a twenty-two-year-old new member of your church. I had a fire inside of me that I did not even know what to do with! It was because you saw my "for such a time as this" moment brewing inside of me and called it forth that I was able to give birth to my life's call, my life's work. I will forever be grateful that you believed in me, prayed for me, and pushed me into my greatness. That fire you helped to ignite is still present and continues to grow some twenty years later! I am so humbled and blessed that God allowed you to be my Mordecai! You did more for me, however, than change my name—you changed my life! I pray that this book can be as much a light on another's path as you have been on mine.

SUSTAINABLE FORESTRY INITIATIVE   Certified Sourcing
www.sfiprogram.org
Label applies to the text stock   SFI-00341

The Pilgrim Press, 700 Prospect Avenue, Cleveland, Ohio 44122
thepilgrimpress.com
© 2012 by Nicole Roberts Jones

Printed in the United States of America on acid-free paper

16   15   14   13   12   5   4   3   2   1

Library of Congress Cataloging-in-Publication Data

Jones, Nicole Roberts, 1969–
    It's your time to shine! : weekly spiritual reflections for women / Nicole Roberts Jones.
    p. cm.
    Includes bibliographical references (p.   ).
    ISBN 978-0-8298-1967-0 (alk. paper)
    1. Christian women—Religious life. 2. Devotional exercises. 3. Spiritual journals—Authorship. I. Title.
BV4527.J6747 2012
242'.643—dc23   2012039358

CONTENTS

INTRODUCTION

Yet who knows whether
you have come . . .
for such a time as this?

—ESTHER 4:14b

The story of Esther reads like a Cinderella story, and it is one of my favorite Bible stories. Born in poverty, orphaned and insignificant, Esther became queen over Persia. Just hearing that makes you wonder how she got from the bottom of the barrel to the top, right? Let me summarize her story so that you will have a full understanding of the woman who lights the path of the journey we shall take together through this book.¹

In a twist of events, Queen Vashti was summoned to appear before her husband, King Ahasuerus, and his ministers at a banquet. The Bible says that she disobeyed her drunk husband because he wanted to parade her around inappropriately in front of everyone. He grew angry over her refusal to obey him, feeling she had embarrassed him in front of his court. Thus he dethroned Vashti as queen and ordered a search for a new queen.

Beautiful young virgins were gathered from all over the land and brought to the palace to compete for the throne, Esther among them. Her uncle Mordecai, who raised her after the death of her parents, worked at the palace. Like any guardian, he wanted the best for his niece and saw a wonderful opportunity for Esther. So he had her birth name, Hadassah, changed to Esther to protect her identity and heritage. Why? A Jewish girl would never be permitted in the palace to be trained as a queen. The young women selected to go through the training were educated and prepared for months before they were ready to meet King Ahasuerus.

Throughout the training process and even during her one night with the king, Esther's humility was markedly different from those around her. This enabled her to be elevated into the position of queen. After becoming queen, Esther was faced with a difficult choice. She was put into a position where she could save her own people from the evil plans of Haman, one of King Ahasuerus' ministers, who hated Jews. Most of all he despised Mordecai because Mordecai refused to bow down to Haman when commanded to do so. Keep in mind, no one knew that Esther was a Jew nor that Mordecai was her uncle. Haman manipulates the king against the Jews and a decree was set for their total destruction. Mordecai then appealed to Esther to use her power and position to save her people:

> For if you keep silence at such a time as this, relief and deliverance will rise for the Jews from another quarter, but you and your father's family will perish. Who knows? Perhaps you have come to the royal dignity for just such a time as this? (Esth. 4:14)

Esther realized that all that has happened in her life had prepared her for this moment, and she gave this response to her uncle:

> Go, gather all the Jews to be found in Susa, and hold a fast on my behalf, and neither eat nor drink for three days, night or day. I and my maids will also fast as you do. After that, I will go to the king, though it is against the law; and if I perish, I perish. (Esth. 4:16)

Obviously Esther was a woman of God, as she asked all the Jews along with her maids to fast and pray for three days as she sought God's direction. Esther knew that she *must* stand in the gap for her people and risk her life by going before the king. What you must understand is that going before the king without being summoned could mean certain death for her. Further, Esther knew she would have to reveal her heritage to the king when she asked him to save the Jews. Only a woman of great faith could trust God in such a frightening situation!

What came to Esther during her time of fasting and prayer was to invite the king and Haman to a series of private banquets.

> On the second day, as they were drinking wine, the king again said to Esther, "What is your petition, Queen Esther? It shall be granted you. And what is your request? Even to the half of my kingdom, it shall be fulfilled." Then Queen Esther answered, "If I have won your favor, O king, and if it pleases the king, let my life be given me—that is my petition—and the lives of my people—that is my request. For we have been sold, I and my people, to be destroyed, to be killed, and to be annihilated. If we had been sold merely as slaves, men and women, I would have held my peace; but no enemy can compensate for this damage to the king." Then King Ahasuerus said to Queen Esther, "Who is he, and where is he, who has presumed to do this?" Esther said, "A foe and enemy, this wicked Haman!" Then Haman was terrified before the king and the queen. (Esth. 7:2–6)

Not only did the king spare Esther's life and that of all the Jews, but he decreed for Haman to be killed on the very gallows Haman had created for Mordecai. We can learn these lessons from Esther's story:

- The hand of God is evident even when we can't see it in the midst of a bad situation.
- God truly uses everything to work together for our good if we can stay focused on and trust in God.
- Esther is a picture of sacrifice as she stood in the gap for her people even at the cost of her own life.

- Esther proved to have a godly and teachable spirit that showed great strength and willing obedience.

- Esther's humility was markedly different from those around her. This brought her favor and enabled her to become queen.

- Esther shows us that remaining respectful and humble, even in difficult if not humanly impossible circumstances, allows us to receive God's blessings!

- Esther's story shows us that we are under God's control and God will work everything together for our good.

- Esther's story shows us that we can be assured that God's plans will not be moved by the actions of evil doers, or those I call "haters"!

We would do well to emulate Esther's godly attitudes in all areas of life, but especially in trials or difficult circumstances. Esther does not complain or show a negative or bad attitude about the situation she is placed in. In fact, throughout the book of Esther, we see that she won the "favor" of those around her. I believe it is God's favor that ultimately led the king to make the choice to save Esther's people. We too can be granted such favor as we learn that "all things work together for good for those who love God, who are called according to [God's] purpose (Rom. 8:28). We must follow Esther's example of trusting God, being positive, humble, and determined to lean on God. Everything you have been through could have been God putting you in a position for *your time to shine.*

This book will focus on how you can achieve your *time-to-shine* moment. How will you do this? There are seven themes (which frame the first seven parts of this book) that will help you see how the aspects of your life are woven together like the tapestry of a fine quilt.

1. BE A WOMAN OF STRENGTH AND DIGNITY—You will learn how to dig deep to understand all of the factors that made Esther a true Proverbs 31 woman. Many women's groups study Proverbs 31. This scripture text illustrates a strong, dignified, hardworking, multifaceted, compassionate, loving, and independent woman who is a great caregiver for her family. As with Esther, this woman's strength in preparation, hardworking nature, and dignity in character bring her to the crossroads of opportunity. Additionally, like the woman in Proverbs 31, Esther has the ability to be faithful and patient despite what is going on around her.

2. KEEP YOUR EYES ON THE PRIZE—We all have a mission in life. Do you know your focus and your goals? Do you know what you are working toward? Are you applying to college, searching for a better job, or starting your own business? Where are you in accomplishing your goal(s)? The key lessons we learn from Esther is the importance of being prepared. I remember hearing my mom say, "God only calls those who are busy." Esther thought she was working hard to become queen. Actually, she was preparing to save her people. Therefore, this part of the book is a call for you to get busy working toward your dreams. It is when you prepare to make your dreams a reality that achievement meets opportunity. You, too, will reach your *time-to-shine* moment.

3. DON'T STAY STUCK—You may have experienced hurt or been hindered by something that stopped you dead in your tracks. Your hurt might have been so deep that it made you no longer believe in your dream, made you think you were not good enough, not smart enough, or not worthy for the thing you desire the most. One of the most beautiful lessons we learn from Esther is that God is present in each and every situation. God will use *everything* for your good. What you must do is muster up enough courage to believe that! Esther did not stay stuck in sorrow. No! Esther did not focus on the problems of yesterday. Esther stayed focused on her tomorrows, her possibilities, and her promise! Therefore, if you are to do and be all that you are meant to in your life, you *cannot* dwell on the negative things that have happened in the past. Likewise, you *cannot* allow negative situations or circumstances to hold you back. You can't allow yourself to stay stuck!

4. KNOW GOD INTIMATELY—Once you know God for yourself, it will be revealed that everything you experienced was just a part of God's greater plan for your life. The only way you can understand this is to wait on God and trust God. How do you trust or believe in someone you do not yet know? The key to knowing God intimately is building and developing your own relationship with God through prayer and fasting. Get to know the unique purpose God has placed in you and allow God's love to pour in and through you. It was ultimately Esther's faith that persuaded her to fast and pray. She knew she needed time with God to gain insight and clarity about what she should do in her moment of great crisis. Esther's life shows the hand of God at work. This can be revealed in your life to usher you into your time-to-shine moment.

5. IRON SHARPENS IRON—When Esther got to her time-to-shine moment, the first thing she did was ask the group of women around her to pray with her. Take a look at the people around you. Can you depend on them to be there for you in your time of need? Are they making positive contributions to your life or are they planting weeds that will ultimately grow up to smother and kill your dreams? Haman planted negative weeds in the king's life, and you see what happened to him. The negative folks gotta go! Only iron can sharpen iron!

6. GIVE TO OTHERS—Remember the African adage, "It takes a village to raise a child"? Well Esther's time-to-shine moment was not to focus on her needs. She unselfishly acted on the need of her village, her people. So what are you doing to give to your village? You can mentor a young person, volunteer to feed the homeless, tutor kids after school, or share your expertise with a local nonprofit. The options are endless for ways you can give so that others may be lifted up. How can you give your gifts as an unselfish act, expecting nothing in return?

7. LET YOUR LIGHT SHINE—The end product of becoming all that you are meant to be is for your light to shine. Esther's light shone as she became queen. It shone the brightest, however, when she rose from being an orphan born in poverty to queen in a palace for the purpose of saving her people. It's time for you to get out there and let the world experience you in all of your splendor! In all of your greatness! When you do, you will shine just as God intended you to. Sure, you may not be called to save your people, as was Esther, but your time-to-shine moment will come when you grow into God's purpose as God created you to do.

I believe that I live in my time-to-shine moment every day as I work with youth, young adults, and women to live into their greatness. I went through many trials and tribulations to get where I am today. Each of the seven areas we explore in this book are from my own journey. My being raised in South Central LA (aka, Los Angeles—think of the movie *Boyz n the Hood*) enabled God to use me to reach back and pull up women from ages eighteen to seventy, so they could find themselves and use their gifts that somehow had been misplaced along the way. My breakthrough came when I began to understand and know for myself—as my favorite Bible verse says—"We know that all things work together for good for those who love God, who are called according to [God's] purpose"—(Rom. 8:28). I can tell you that once I stopped allowing others to write my story and I picked up a pen to author what defines my life by *knowing* me and *growing* me, a fundamental shift happened in my life! Now this *joy*, this abundance, this bliss that I have is what I desire for every woman, and that is why I do what I do and why this book is in your hands right now. I pray that these seven themes will be as much of a blessing in your life as they have been in mine.

Throughout the journey of this book, we focus on each of these seven themes over the course of fifty weeks. At the end of each week, I leave you with a thought to ponder. At the end of each week, I encourage you to take the time to explore the week's lessons as well as any other thoughts that come up for you. Utilize the space provided in the book as well as a personal journal so that you can truly take time for intimacy (what I like to call "into-me-see").

The more you explore, the greater you will grow. Most books give you a topic per day, but I encourage you to use a weekly theme so that you can fully explore each topic before moving to the next. You will see how this personal time will water the seed that is already within you. How do I know there is a seed in you? Well, that seed is what I believe is our gift, our purpose, our life's calling that God planted in us when God created us. It is that seed that you will water and see grow over the course of our time together in this book, so that you too will come to your time-to-shine moment!

The last two weeks of our year together will offer an opportunity for you to explore the lessons you have learned about yourself over the previous fifty weeks. It will be a time to explore what you have learned to find as your strength, to see how you have built up your weakest areas, and to really give you a perspective of where you are now and where you are going. The goal is that when you emerge at the end of fifty-two weeks with this book, you have become a more vigorous, amazing, empowered, brilliant, fabulous, phenomenal, dazzling YOU!

Let's make this the best year ever! Let's get deliberate about growing our greatness! Let's live our lives in our purpose lane, moving toward our dreams, our goals, our desires! Let's get focused on the lessons that life brings that make us better, stronger, wiser—so that we too can get to our time-to-shine moment!

PART ONE

Be a Woman of Strength and Dignity

WEEK 1

When Preparation Meets Opportunity

I believe the greatest lesson that we learn from Esther is what can happen when *preparation meets opportunity.* When we learn to move past our fear and allow faith to be our guide, all things are possible. Just think about it—we have had an opportunity to witness Esthers among us!

How about when Rosa Parks sat in the front of that bus? Do you think Rosa Parks thought when she defied the Jim Crow laws of the South that her tired determination would begin a movement?

Or how about Dr. Martin Luther King Jr. and the launch of the civil rights movement? Do you think Dr. King, at the age of twenty-four and a newly appointed pastor to a church in Selma, Alabama, thought he would be called to a meeting and be elected president of the Montgomery Improvement Association? Yet his election sparked the Montgomery bus boycott. It was the match that lit the fire to the civil rights movement.

Or how about Ms. Oprah when she started that little TV show or, later, her own network? Do you think when she began her career as a reporter in Baltimore, making approximately $22,000 a year, that she envisioned hosting her own television show and then becoming the first woman to own a network? Do you think she thought that she would lead a movement for people to "Live Their Best Lives"?

Or consider even President Barack Obama. Do you think when he was working as a community organizer on Chicago's South Side that he knew his grassroots work would enable him to become the first African American president of the United States?

I can go on and on; the point is that those individuals and countless others were prepared when opportunity came to their doorstep. So how do *you* get prepared? By living each day fully present, working at your *maximum* potential toward your purpose, your dream, and your goal(s) so that when you are faced with opportunity, you are ready to move forward. Get prepared by doing phenomenal work today as you wait with happy anticipation for tomorrow. This may be at your current job until you get the breakthrough to start your own business or make the right contact for the next position. Or it could mean going back to school, buying that home. Whatever that may be, you should have your own goals, desires, and dreams. It means that you should do all that you can to move in the direction of your gifts, your hopes, and your dreams, which all will be a byproduct of your greatness.

Working in a preparatory spirit also calls you to keep your focus, determination, and perseverance and not become distracted or diverted. It means that when preparation meets opportunity, you too will have your very own time-to-shine moment. Truthfully, I believe we each *will* come to our very own time-to-shine moment.

THIS WEEK THE QUESTION for you to ponder is, are you prepared? Or are you taking steps toward preparation? Each day, what can you do to move in the direction of your gifts, your hopes, your dreams, and your greatness? (Use the following space or a journal to write down your answers.)

WEEK 2

You Will Wait

Another great lesson we learn from Esther is timing. Esther definitely understood the importance of timing. She was not in a hurry but instead remained prayerful until it was the absolute right time to have the life-or-death conversation with her husband. She had the quiet patience to wait until the perfect moment to do what she needed to do. I would liken this act of timing and patience to that of a dancer. For a dancer knows when to wait and when to move. Think of this concept through the eyes of, say, an Alvin Ailey dancer; it is feeling the music speak to your spirit and allowing the fluidity of what you feel within that translates into movement. You never see a professional dancer looking at his or her fellow dancers in anticipation of the next move. Instead, the dancer waits patiently in a pose until the exact moment to move. This beautiful relationship of time and movement is exactly what we witness in the story of Esther, but Ms. Esther even takes this moment of waiting to a whole new level.

How? Well what does Esther do while she waits for the right time to have her critical conversation with the king? This woman throws a dinner party for her husband. Esther does not sit around sad and anxious. She is patient, trusting God, and setting the atmosphere for when that small voice inside of her (some of us call this voice intuition or our gut feeling, but I call that little voice God) says, the stage is set and it's time to have the conversation.

Remember, the conversation that Esther had with the king could have led to her death! You see, coming before the king without being summoned—even to invite him to dinner!—could be punishable by death. Furthermore, the king did not know his wife was a Jew. Yes, she had held that secret from him, and now she was going to ask him to spare her life and the life of *all* the Jews! I don't know about you, but if I had a life-or-death situation in my hands like this, I would find it hard to wait gracefully. Esther did not act rashly. She didn't sit and begin figuring things out, she waited until her spirit told her that the time had come. What I take away from Esther's ability to gracefully wait is this:

- *Trust God.* Equally as important as what you are waiting to do is what is happening that you cannot see. This is the work God is doing to line up the absolute perfect time for you to have that important conversation with your spouse or partner, your supervisor, or whomever. If you dive in and have that conversation without waiting for the perfect time, you could mess up everything. The Bible verse I absolutely love here is "The king's heart is a stream of water in the hand of the Lord; he turns it wherever he will" (Prov. 21:1). Wow, God is always working behind the scenes for us. God lines up every perfect person, place, or thing! If you can focus on God and not the situation, you can learn to have faith instead of fear. You can trust instead of doubt. You can have quiet assurance instead of losing heart!

- *Have patience.* Timing can sometimes be more important than taking action. It is important not only that you act, but that you act at the absolute right time. Yes, learning how to be graceful while having to wait is key. It is not rolling your neck at folks because you are not getting your way, or rolling your eyes, or being mad. So if you absolutely *hate* your job but you know in your gut it is not time to quit, be the *best* employee you can be. Patience means learning to smile in the face of frustration and trusting that the time will come, and you'll know when the definite, perfect time is to act.

- Look for the open door or window. It's interesting that sometimes people wait and wait and then when the opportunity is set before them, they do nothing. So when that door swings open, *you must act!* Don't doubt yourself, become afraid, and do nothing. Sometimes you are only given one open door to walk through, so don't lose the opportunity because of fear. When a person is placed in your path to bless you and is willing to help you to begin your new business, *you must act!* If you get laid off, look for the open window of opportunity—it's coming! If your mate leaves, look for the open window of opportunity. No, do not jump out of the window(!), but wait for God to bless you with your soulmate. Wait and then go through that open door that God will open before you.

In her book *Lanterns,* Marian Wright Edelman said it best: "God chooses the actors, the times, the places, sets the stage, lifts the curtain, and begins the drama. Our task is to be ready to play our parts and to do the work God assigns us without anxiety according to the strengths and gifts we are given."[2]

THE THOUGHT TO PONDER for week two is, in what ways can you build up your patience "muscle"? How can you increase your ability to trust God and wait on God's perfect timing? (Use the following space or a journal to write down your answers and thoughts.)

WEEK 3

—

Let's Call Her Strength and Dignity

There is a Bible verse that I think perfectly sums up all that we have discussed thus far about Esther: "Strength and dignity are her clothing, and she laughs at the time to come" (Prov. 31:25).

When I think of Esther, I think of the quiet assurance that she resonated in "such a time as this." She knew who she was and, more importantly, she knew who God was! If I were to translate Esther into a woman of today, I would describe her as a strong, dignified, Bible toting, multitasking, compassionate, independent woman. This is a woman who can run her own business or classroom or is the director of a department with staff that report to her. At the same time, she is also a partner to her husband or significant other, and she does her part at home as much as she does at the office. When a problem arises at the office or at home, she does not panic. She trusts God and lets go and lets God. She lets go while she gracefully smiles in the face of fear, knowing that all things work together for God's good and this too will be sorted out and handled in a timely and appropriate manner.

The woman I just described is really the Proverbs 31 woman. For those of you who have never heard of or read about the virtuous woman in Proverbs 31, take a moment to read it. Proverbs 31:11–31 offers an empowering look at the role of women. Notice how this virtuous woman parallels Esther:

> The heart of her husband trusts in her, and he will have
> no lack of gain. She does him good, and not harm, all the

days of her life. She seeks wool and flax, and works with willing hands. She is like the ships of the merchant, she brings her food from far away. She rises while it is still night and provides food for her household and tasks for her servantgirls. She considers a field and buys it; with the fruit of her hands she plants a vineyard. She girds herself with strength, and makes her arms strong. She perceives that her merchandise is profitable. Her lamp does not go out at night. She puts her hands to the distaff, and her hands hold the spindle. She opens her hand to the poor, and reaches out her hands to the needy. She is not afraid for her household when it snows, for all her household are clothed in crimson. She makes herself coverings; her clothing is fine linen and purple. Her husband is known in the city gates, taking his seat among the elders of the land. She makes linen garments and sells them; she supplies the merchant with sashes. Strength and dignity are her clothing, and she laughs at the time to come.

She opens her mouth with wisdom, and the teaching of kindness is on her tongue. She looks well to the ways of her household, and does not eat the bread of idleness. Her children rise up and call her happy; her husband too, and he praises her: "Many women have done excellently, but you surpass them all." Charm is deceitful, and beauty is vain, but a woman who fears the Lord is to be praised. Give her a share in the fruit of her hands, and let her works praise her in the city gates.

This indeed is what Esther represents, and this description helps to provide a guide for each of us as we define ourselves as employee, employer, or performer; as wife, girlfriend, or fiancée; as mother, auntie, sister, or grandmother. Esther shows us that there is no problem too big for God, and she shows how to handle it all with style and grace. Now, that is the woman I aspire to be!

There are so many women in history, past and present, who would fall into the Proverbs 31 category. Women like First Lady Michelle Obama, who is independent, strong, and focused and who cares about family values. This is definitely a woman who puts family first while also making her mark—all with style and grace! So as we take this moment to think of Proverbs 31 and the real life of virtuous women, I charge you to step up your own game (yes, *me too*). Step up your game to be the woman God designed you to be, a woman of strength.

A Strong Woman vs. a Woman of Strength[3]

A strong woman works out every day,
Pride in her appearance she portrays,
But a woman of strength kneels to pray,
Her soul in shape, God leading the way.

A strong woman claims she isn't afraid of anything,
Looking forward to challenges each day will bring,
Women of strength show courage in the midst of fear,
Declaring triumph through faith because God is near.

Strong women won't let anyone get the best of them,
So skilled in defenses even if they have to pretend,
Yet a woman of strength gives her best to everyone,
And even on a cloud filled day still bright as the sun. . . .

A strong woman walks head first with no doubt in her mind,
No matter what, she'll not make this mistake a second time,
But a woman of strength knows God will catch her when she falls,
So when a situation arises again, she's not afraid to answer
*   the call. . . .*

A strong woman has faith that for the journey she'll have enough,
No matter how uneven the terrain or roads being rocky and
*   rough,*

A woman of strength knows it's in the journey she will become strong,
And the love of God is forever with her, no matter how difficult or long. . . .

Let's all work toward being women of strength and dignity! Together we all walk in this journey as a village of women moving toward living in our *maximum! Maximum* hope, *maximum* opportunity, *maximum* love, *maximum* possibility, *maximum* purpose—women living in our *maximum potential!*

THE QUESTION TO PONDER this week is, in what ways are you a woman of strength and dignity? In what areas might you need to move priorities around in your life in order to increase your focus on you and amplify your strength for yourself and your family? (Use the following space or a journal to write down your answers and thoughts.)

WEEK 4

LOVE AND SACRIFICE

Esther's story is definitely one of love and sacrifice. But just what is love?

> Love is patient; love is kind; love is not envious or boastful or arrogant or rude. It does not insist on its own way; it is not irritable or resentful; it does not rejoice in wrongdoing, but rejoices in the truth. It bears all things, believes all things, hopes all things, endures all things. Love never ends. But as for prophecies, they will come to an end; as for tongues, they will cease; as for knowledge, it will come to an end. (1 Cor. 13:4–8)

The main take-away from Esther's story is that love is something that transcends self; love wants what is best for the one you love. It is an act of selflessness. It is the mother who goes without so her children can have what they need. It is the friend who forgoes a promotion so that her friend will not end up standing in the unemployment line. It is the sister who—although she has a very important business meeting in the morning—stays up all night to help nurse you through a cold.

To take this a step further, to *love* someone is not about you. It is about the other person. So where does sacrifice come in? To sacrifice is to give up something you really want for the benefit of someone else. Now, it is not truly sacrifice if you are pouting about it or upset. It is sacrifice when you are happy to do it without needing to be acknowledged for it. This indeed is what we see in Esther's story. When Esther hears what Haman has planned for her people, she says: "I will go to the king, though it is against the law; and if I perish, I perish" (Esth. 4:16b). This part of this story tells us a lot about this woman. It tells us that she knows this moment in time is not about her but is an opportunity to look beyond self and do something that will benefit her people. Esther does not make a public announcement about it. She goes into her chamber and prays. She comes out and throws a dinner party for the king! Esther is thinking exclusively about the good of her people. She is not concerned that she might die doing this. She is looking beyond self, to do what is right. Yes, she indeed may have been put in this place "for such a time as this."

So, to celebrate love, we must first take an introspective look and love ourselves in order to freely love someone else. We must first love ourselves in order to create an environment of love in a marriage, in a home, with family and friends, or whatever this may mean for you in this moment. It is relishing how love and sacrifice go hand in hand. Sacrifice itself is an act born out of love, done not because you see other people doing it or because you are going to get something out of it. It is done simply because you love the person so much that you want to see what is best for that person happen.

Love is not about keeping a list of all the things you have done for someone and reminding them of it, nor is it keeping a list of all the ways someone has done you wrong. After all, making these lists does not come from a place of love. Instead it keeps a cloud of negativity looming. If you have to remind people what you have done for them or what they have done to you, the question is, why is this person in your life? Love is accepting people for who they are while expecting them to be the best for themselves. Love delights in what is good and lets go of that all too familiar phrase, "what about me?"

NOW, WHAT ABOUT YOU? How can we enhance our ability to love while learning how to give of ourselves for the benefit of others? The thought to ponder this week is, first and foremost, do you fully love you? Before you can love anyone else you must love yourself first. The next question to tackle is what does selfless love look like to you.(Use the following space or a journal to answer.)

Only when we give joyfully, without hesitation
or thought of gain, can we truly know what love means.
—LEO BUSCAGLIA

Love is more than three words mumbled
before bedtime. Love is sustained by action, a pattern of
devotion in the things we do for each other every day.
—NICHOLAS SPARKS

For anything worth having one must pay the price; and the price is
always work, patience, love, self-sacrifice—no paper currency,
no promises to pay, but the gold of real service.
—JOHN BURROUGHS

When people get caught up with that which is right
and they are willing to sacrifice for it,
there is no stopping point short of victory.
—MARTIN LUTHER KING JR.

Love is friendship set on fire.
—AUTHOR UNKNOWN

PART TWO

Keep Your Eyes on the Prize

WEEK 5

I Won't Take Nothin' for My Journey Now

The phrase "keep your eyes on the prize" makes me think of my ancestors. The prize for them was *freedom*, and, after they received that prize, they then set their eyes on obtaining *education*, and *equal rights*, and being able to sit and eat at the same table or counter as European Americans. Think about it, your ancestors—whether you are of African, Latin, Caribbean, Asian, Jewish, Italian, Irish, German, European, or other descent—did what they did for the benefit of others who would follow them. They had to fight hard to obtain the American dream. You owe your existence to their legacy. The greatest way to pay homage to your ancestors is for you to maximize all the hope and opportunity you can.

So what legacy will we leave for those who come behind us? What are we doing to light the path for the next generation? What is the shining example your life will give to others? Well, your light really does shine when you maximize your potential. "In the same way, let your light shine before others, so that they may see your good works and give glory to your Father in heaven" (Matt. 5:16). In order to shine you must consider *what is your prize, your gift, your goal, your purpose?* What are you aiming to do or to be? Each goal we meet along our own individual path in life is why our ancestors fought, so that we could have hope and opportunity. As we begin to reflect on this over the next few weeks, our first stop along this path is to pay homage to our ancestors.

"Keep your eyes on the prize" is the title of a folk song that became influential during the American civil rights movement.

The chorus to the song goes like this: "Hold on, hold on, keep your eyes on the prize, hold on, hold, on."[4]
So take a look at your life's journey and, in so doing, look at where you are now and where you seek to go. Yes, as you work toward getting there, your light shines! This indeed defines our prize. The prize is the realization of your goal(s). Esther thought her goal was to become queen and, boy, oh boy, did she have an even bigger goal to reach after she became queen. The point is, in order to become *all* that God would have you be, you have to work toward something! So what are you working toward? What is your goal? Is it a better job or to start a company? To buy a new home? To get a raise or make more money? To become more physically fit? A better relationship or to be in a relationship? *This is a call for you to define where you are and begin to look at where it is you choose to go.* Your prize is the *realization* of becoming all you dream of being. It is you taking hold of the hope and opportunity your ancestors fought for. It is staying true to who God is and what you were put on this earth to do or to be. How does this inform your vision of who you are on the way to where you are going?

ONE OF MY FAVORITE LINES in the song "Keep Your Eyes on the Prize" says, "I wouldn't take nothin' for my journey now." This is the week's reflection quote. So plot your journey by writing down in the following space or in a journal all the dreams and goals you have for yourself.

WEEK 6

—

WRITE THE VISION

I hope last week was enlightening as you worked on defining your goals and/or your dreams. So why did I suggest you do this work? Why did you "write the vision; make it plain on tablets" (Hab. 2:2a)?

The purpose is to declare your vision and confirm it by writing it out. It is a way of giving substance to the things you hope for by taking them out of your head and making them visual on paper. How you take this work of making your goals/prize list to the next level is by creating a vision board.

A vision board is a visual representation of the things you want to do or be. It is gathering pictures that will enable you to *see* your dream(s) laid out before you as a reminder of where you are headed; it will help you to help you stay focused. How do you create your vision board? Find or buy a large piece of construction paper, a bulletin board, or something the size of poster board. Gather magazines or newspapers and cut out pictures, symbols, and words that represent what you want to do or be. Glue these onto your paper or board. After it is completed, place it in a strategic place where you can view it every day. It is just that simple. My vision board is made of pictures and phrases that I cut out of magazines.

Creating a vision board will help you to "keep your eyes on the prize." I have heard it put this way: Vision boards program the reticular activating system (RAS) of your brain, which plays a vital part in your ability to achieve goals. How?

Imagine that you're walking through a noisy airport. Think of all the noise—hundreds of people talking, music, announcements, luggage carriers. How much of this noise is brought to your attention? Not a lot. True, you can hear general background noise, but not many of us bother to listen to each individual sound. But then an announcement comes over the PA system—saying your name or maybe your flight. Suddenly your attention is full on. Your RAS is the automatic mechanism inside your brain that brings relevant information to your attention. . . . You can deliberately program the reticular activating system by choosing the exact messages you send from your conscious mind. For example, you can set goals, or say affirmations, or visualize your goals.[5]

So if you can choose what you want to send to your subconscious mind and you know that your subconscious mind works in pictures and images, then you want to create a vision board that will propel what you desire into reality.

In other words, you want to call "into existence the things that do not exist" (Rom. 4:17b). Once you make this board for yourself, hang it in a place where you will be reminded of your vision on a daily basis. My board is in my office, right in front of my desk, where I have to look up at it every day. It reminds me of where I am headed and is something that helps me stay focused on my own prize. Why should we do this? "Where there is no vision the people perish" (Prov. 29:18 KJV).

How I interpret this is that if we have no direction, we have no purpose. It's like driving a car with no determined destination, and what's the point of doing that?! We all must have a prize to set our mind toward and to work toward. Therefore, your vision board helps you keep your focus as you set sail on the future of your dreams. It does not matter how young or old you are. You can use a tool to concentrate on what you want to accomplish! You are on the road of life, aren't you? Where are you headed?

I will go into depth about the purpose of creating this vision board and what it can manifest in your life next week, but for now, be happy creating your vision, your purpose, your prize board.

Be creative! Your possibilities are endless!

THIS WEEK TAKE YOUR WORK beyond this book and create your vision board!

WEEK 7

—

IT'S LIKE A BOOMERANG

So you have done your lists and made your vision board . . . now what? As I touched on last week, the purpose of the vision board is to make a visual representation of the things you want to do and/or be. Making a vision board is a way to initiate what is called the "law of attraction." The law of attraction states that you attract anything that you give attention to . . . it is again best explained by the information filtering system of your brain—the RAS touched on last week. In essence, your vision board begins to help you to stay focused; it helps you to keep your thoughts set on your dream so that, "as a [woman] thinks in [her] heart, so is [s]he" (Prov. 23:7 NKJV).

Your vision board starts the process of working to get your dreams, thoughts, and actions in alignment so that when they all line up together, they will produce your dream. When you throw out a boomerang, it comes right back. You are the author of your own destiny just by the thoughts you choose. Yes, you have the power to choose faith or to doubt the vision we have for your future. Hmmm . . . what I am saying is that the mind is the master hub of your inner thoughts and the outer enactment of your thoughts, which equals what gets played out in your life. So if you can get your thoughts in alignment with who God says you are and what your prize is to be, then you are well on your way to the path where you will receive it.

You must "be transformed by the renewing of your minds . . ." (Rom. 12:2).

So if up until now your thoughts have produced doubt and insecurity, you can make a choice that they now will produce faith and assurance. If up until now your thoughts produced hesitation and uncertainty, you can make a choice that they now will produce belief and confidence. As the apostle Paul says, "I am confident of this, that the one who began a good work among you will bring it to completion . . . ." (Phil. 1:6).

Here is a story that just might illustrate this a bit better. Ruth Krauss's children's book *The Carrot Seed* is about a little boy who planted a carrot seed. His mother said, "I am afraid it won't come up." His father said, "I'm afraid it won't come up." And his big brother said, "I am afraid it won't come up." Every day the little boy pulled up the weeds around the seed and sprinkled the ground with water. But nothing came up. But he still pulled up the weeds around it every day and sprinkled the ground with water. And then, one day, a carrot came up just as the little boy had known it would."[6]

Seeds do not grow over night, but take time and nurturing. So it takes confidence and trust, even after you plant the seed of your prize. It is *faith* that will give you the wherewithal to water it and water it and water it, even when you do not see anything coming forth. Then one day all of that determination, focus, and hard work produces your *prize!* It definitely takes patience and perseverance to hang in there through the days when you see nothing happening to make your dream come to fruition in your life. It takes faith and perseverance, but if you hang in there, keep your eyes on the prize, and only do, say, or think those things that are in alignment with your prize, then eventually, one day, you will indeed reap what you have sown.

However, if you let time, circumstance, or unbelief cause you to doubt what God has put in you, you will be like the children of Israel walking around the same mountain for forty years, going nowhere near the promised land! If God has placed something special in you, don't you think God wants to see you get there?

Yet God leaves determination and will up to us. Therefore, if over time you let weeds grow, get frustrated, and give up, or you let your friends talk you out of your dream, you definitely will not see the prize move from visual to reality. *Whatever you throw out (the boomerang) is what will come back to you.* As we move next week into charting your course to get to your prize, you must stop in this place along the way to push your thoughts and character into alignment with your prize.

"As a woman thinketh in her heart, so is she."

HERE'S WHAT TO PONDER THIS WEEK: What's in your heart? What thoughts and actions are you sending out, and are thus coming back to you like a boomerang? (Write these down in the following space or in your journal.)

WEEK 8

—

Program Your GPS

Now that you have defined your prize and made your vision board, it is time to chart your course, in essence, to plan out how you are going to get to the destination of your prize—the goals or dreams you have for your life. Anytime I need direction, my absolute favorite thing to use is my GPS (global positioning system). So as you begin to chart your course, why not use your own personal GPS to plan out your directions to get to your prize. For us, the GPS would mean:

- Get to the goal
- Planning
- Steps

What will your path be so that you will arrive at the destination of your prize? It is time to spell out the steps you must take to arrive at your destination, and, to do so, you must do the necessary planning and research so that you can create action steps to follow.

When God told Noah to build the ark, do you think Noah just started building? No, Noah had to make a plan to build the ark, he had to decide what to do, in what order to do it, how to do it, and when to do it, so that he could get to the place of a finished work—the ark. Well, now that you have written out your goal, your prize, your vision—your ark—it's time to plot out your plan. How will you obtain your prize? What is your course of action? Now's the time to begin to plan what you need to do to get to your destination of choice. Start by breaking down your plan into small steps to accomplish one at a time. So take a moment and answer these questions for yourself:

MY PLAN	STEPS TO COMPLETE
Within the next year, *I seek to accomplish _____.* *What do I need to do to get there?*	
Within the next five years, *I seek to accomplish _____.* *What do I need to do to get there?*	
EDUCATION: *If I need or want to go back to school,* *what do I need to do to get there?*	
HEALTH: *What am I aiming to achieve?*	
CAREER: *What am I aiming to achieve?*	
MONEY: *How much do I want to earn and by when?*	
RELATIONSHIPS: (family and friends, significant other/romance) *What do I want?*	
PERSONAL GROWTH: *Are my thoughts holding me back? Are my actions* *holding me back? If so, set a goal here to make* *changes that will help you reach your prize.*	

Take each portion of your vision and plan out the action steps you must take to get there. Use only positive language when you are writing out your actions steps; remember what we talked about: "As a woman thinketh in her heart, so is she" (Prov. 23:7 NKJV, adapted). You must believe in "the God . . . who . . . calls into existence the things that do not exist" (Rom. 4:17b).

So if we are going to be in line with both of these ways of thinking, we must line up our words and/or language to help us move in a positive direction. In addition, make sure you set SMART goals: **S**pecific, **M**easurable, **A**ttainable, **R**ealistic, and **T**ime-focused.

Be as specific as possible; write in dates, times, and amounts so that you can define what you need to do as much as possible as well as measure your achievement. For instance, instead of saying, "I want to go back to school," say, "I want to complete a degree in higher education by 2014," or be even more specific and write down what degree you hope to complete (nursing, business, biology, whatever). Set priorities. What do you need to accomplish first, second, third? This may seem a bit overwhelming, but *take it one step at a time*. I am sure Noah did not hear from God and then just start building the ark; after all, he had not done this before. He had to research and figure it all out, and you can do the same thing. Just start by putting all the things you want to accomplish on a piece of paper, and list out the action steps you need to take under each item. If you don't know what to do to accomplish some of your steps, this is where you need to do some research. Once you write down all the action steps under each item, you can then begin to look at what you need to accomplish first, second, and so on.

Why are we taking so much time to plan and get prepared? Well, if Esther is our guide, the greatest lesson that we learn from Esther is what can happen when *preparation meets opportunity*. Esther herself went through twelve months of *preparation* just to have an *opportunity* to be considered for queen. And then if she hadn't been prepared prior to that dinner meeting with the king, then the next *very* important moment of opportunity—the moment where she saved her people from being destroyed—never would have happened. Now while we may not become a woman who will stand in the gap for our people, God has called each of us uniquely to do or to be something, and that is what is on your vision board. Ultimately, you are doing this work so that when your preparation meets opportunity, you will be ready. You too will have your very own "time-to-shine moment." *It's time to make those plans! Program that GPS!*

"Good planning and hard work lead to prosperity, but hasty shortcuts lead to poverty" (Prov. 21:5 NLT).

"Wise people think before they act; fools don't—and even brag about their foolishness" (Prov. 13:16 NLT).

THIS WEEK YOUR ACTION is to actually go back to the table and write out your SMART goals (specific, measurable, attainable, realistic, and time-focused) for every area of your life!

WEEK 9

—

Ask for Directions

Regarding our last week's topic, as you all work to chart your course there will be areas that you may find complicated, challenging, or confusing. It is in these moments that you need guidance and/or support so that you can get to your desired destination. The best thing for you to do when you find yourself in this place is to stop and *ask for directions.*

Now, I am sure you wouldn't ask for directions from someone who has never been to your destination of choice. After all, why would you ask for directions from someone who might get you lost? With this in mind, you want to find someone who can give you wise counsel and levelheaded insight, someone who will help you move in the direction of your prize. If your GPS loses its signal, you have that someone who can point you in the right direction. That person can help you sort through and find the signal again that will help you stay on the course toward your prize.

Why should we seek direction? Even Jesus' mother, Mary, needed direction. When the angel came to tell her that she would become pregnant with Jesus, do you think she automatically knew what to do? No, she needed direction! In that same visit where the angel told Mary that she was going to have a son, the angel then—perhaps sensing that Mary needed a little support and guidance—told Mary, "And now, your relative Elizabeth in her old age has also conceived a son; and this is the sixth month for her who was said to be barren" (Luke 1:36).

So what did Mary do? She went and spent three months with a woman who was also carrying a miracle. Elizabeth's miracle was not quite the same as Mary's, but she could definitely understand what Mary was going through, as she had already been dealing with it for some time herself. Elizabeth, like no one else, could help Mary in her current course of action. Elizabeth could provide her with support and encouragement, and, more than anything, Mary knew that Elizabeth was already on the road she too must travel. What better person could provide Mary with sound direction? It was during Mary's visit with her cousin Elizabeth that Mary came to terms with her prize, becoming the mother of Jesus.

You might ask, why is this story included? Well, we are all pregnant with our own purpose and there is definitely someone out there who can understand where you are headed. So don't be afraid to stop and ask for directions as you chart your course. Ask directions from a trusted mentor, pastor, friend, sister, mother. Whoever it might be, find that person who will help you to find your own way! When Mary visited with her cousin Elizabeth, it lead her from doubt to confidence, from weakness to strength, from facing her future with fear to facing her future with faith. If you want to read the whole story of Mary and her visit with Elizabeth, check out Luke 1:26–56. One of my favorite verses in this story is Luke 1:37, which says, "For nothing will be impossible with God."

Therefore, know that obtaining your prize is definitely possible! All you need to do is to effectively set out on your path toward getting there. Reach out and get the help you need to get where you need to go. If you need to ask for directions, by all means, *ask!* The point I am making is that you should not feel like you have to know everything. Sometimes you have to seek guidance and insight from trusted counsel. Sometimes you may need to seek encouragement and support so that you will not grow weary and lose heart. And if you never reach out to those torch bearers on your path, you will never get what you need for your journey. So, ladies, when and if you need it, *stop and ask for directions!*

WHO ARE SOME FOLKS YOU ALREADY KNOW who can help you in your journey toward identifying the greatness within you? Write down their names. Then, this week, reach out to your network by phone or e-mail. Ask each person on your list to be a mentor on your journey. The absolute worst thing anyone can do is say no, and it does not hurt to ask. Right? You never know how someone can bless you until you ask.

Successful people turn everyone who
can help them into mentors!
—JOHN CROSBY

He who is afraid of asking is ashamed of learning.
—DANISH PROVERB

WEEK 10

—

BEGIN WITH THE END IN MIND

Now that you have made your plans and asked for directions as needed, it is time for you to get ready to put your plan to action before we discuss how to put your car in drive next week. Before we get into gear, however, the most important nugget I can share with you is that we *must* begin with the end in mind. Stephen Covey says,

> All things are created twice. There's a mental or first creation, and a physical or second creation of all things. . . . You have to make sure that the blueprint, the first creation, is really what you want, that you've thought everything through. Then you put it into bricks and mortar. Each day you go to the construction shed and pull out the blueprint to get marching orders for the day. You begin with the end in mind.[7]

Your charge from this day forward is to begin with the end in mind as you move in the direction of your prize. I am sure you have seen how construction workers begin with the end in mind by utilizing their blueprint, which they look at often as they work. *Well, consider yourself under construction!* You see, the course you have set has now become your blueprint toward building your prize, your vision, your goals. Therefore, you must refer to your blueprint often as you are constructing and/or building the future of your dreams. This is how you begin with the end in mind, so as you look at your blueprint or vision board, you formulate things on your to-do list to get things done. This may occur daily, weekly or monthly. I suggest you do this at least weekly but how often is totally up to you. Looking at your blueprint to-do list will help you to see what you have completed each week as you check things off and what needs to happen next. Be sure to check off completed items so you can see the progress you are making; this helps you to actually see the headway you are making toward constructing your prize!

In week 6 when you wrote your vision, I referred to Habakkuk 2:2a: "Write the vision; make it plain on tablets. Now let me share the second part of that verse about writing your vision: "so that a runner may read it." The obvious meaning is to write clearly and large enough so that someone running by can still read it. But consider the expression "running with it." Like when you are at a meeting and someone thinks of a new idea or concept to work on? Well if you are running with it, you are making it happen, you are announcing to the world what your goal is, and you are staying focused on getting to it at all costs. In essence what we are doing is similar to what Paul said to the Philippians: "I press on toward the goal for the prize of the heavenly call of God in Christ Jesus" (Phil. 3:14).

What we need to do is focus on running straight toward our prize, our vision, our goal. With God's help, we will not let anything distract us from it as we stay focused on it, as we *begin with the end in mind!* Or as we *keep our eyes on the prize!*

HERE'S YOUR WORK FOR THIS WEEK. As we prepare to drive forward, refer to your blueprint on an ongoing basis, make to-do lists, cross things off as you complete them, and then make new lists as you refer to your blueprint. Begin with the end in mind! The question to ponder for this week is, in what ways will I begin with the end in mind?

Winning starts with beginning.
—ROBERT H. SCHULLER

Mighty things from small beginnings grow.
—JOHN DRYDEN

A journey of a thousand miles begins with a single step.
—CHINESE PROVERB

WEEK 11

PUT YOUR CAR IN DRIVE

Now that we have made our vision boards and mapped out our plan toward getting there, it is time to put your car in drive. It is time to actually work on the task you have laid out for yourself. After all, "faith apart from works is barren" (James 2:20).

So you must do the work if you want to see your vision manifest in your life. What's the point in having a vision and making a plan if you are not going to work the plan? It's kind of like a person praying for a job, but never sending out a resume. How do you expect to obtain your prize if you do absolutely nothing to get it? This is a call for the P's—perform, pursue, and persist.

Perform! It is time to take action. *Start now!* It is the momentum of movement that is important. Do not sit idle.

Pursue! You must be aggressive. Get on the road and make it happen! After all, how do you expect to get there if you never put your car in gear? Step on the gas!!

Persist! You must be determined, unshakable, and unmovable in the pursuit of your vision! Persistence and commitment are absolutely necessary to achieve anything in life!

These three P's are how you put your car in drive to move in the direction of your prize. You know, when I was little, my mother always told me that actions speak louder than words. I am sure many of you have also heard this saying. I never quite understood what she meant until I was old enough to act on those words in my own life. We can talk about something until we are blue in the face, but unless we are actually doing what we talk about, our words mean absolutely nothing! The following Bible verse also ap-plies: "You will know them by their fruits" (Matt. 7:16).

What fruit will you bear? This refers to the conversation of harvest as we planted the seed of our prize in week 7. Now is the time to perform, pursue, and persist in the watering, which is your call to action! Get out there and *do it!* Put those wheels in motion and begin to move in the direction of your prize!

THIS WEEK THINK ABOUT what you must do to set your wheels in motion. What do you need to do to put your car in drive in pursuit of all you are meant to be?

Even if you are on the right track,
you'll get run over if you just sit there.
—WILL ROGERS

Either move or be moved.
—COLIN POWELL

Trust only movement. Life happens at the level
of events, not of words. Trust movement.
—ALFRED ADLER

Action is the last resource of those
who know not how to dream.
—OSCAR WILDE

WEEK 12

—

STOP AT THE REST STOP

I remember taking long road trips when I was little and how my parents had to stop at rest stops. As a child, I absolutely hated stopping at those rest stops because I was anxious to reach our destination! As an adult, I now understand why we stopped. My father, the driver, had to stop to get a little rest after being cramped in the car for so long. He had to stop because when he would get tired, he might start driving in a way that lacked clarity and focus. Honey, when my father was like that, his head would begin nodding. It was at those rest stops that my father could regain his focus. When it was time to get back on the road, everyone was happy and focused. We would sing and smile. Often, my father would find a whole new route that would help us get to our destination faster—all because he stopped at the rest stops along the way.

Taking a moment to stop and see where you are and to gain your focus will help you see your direction in a whole new perspective. What I did not realize then that I realize now as an adult is that, at those rest stops, my father was actually tapping into the peace within. That is what I call that space for only you and God. What I realize is that this moment gave him clarity and focus as he stopped to take a breather and renew himself for our journey. This is something we all must do as we travel toward our prize. When you grow tired and weary, instead of giving up, stop. Pull over. Spend some time at the rest stops along the way so frustration and exhaustion do not infiltrate your pursuit and so weariness and disappointment do not take you off course. As Paul said to the church at Galatia, "So let us not grow weary in doing what is right, for we will reap at harvest time, if we do not give up" (Gal. 6:9).

On this journey, take time to *stop at the rest stop* and gain focus. Rest and look around so that you may gain insight for what you need to do next. *This moment of rest is just as important as the journey itself!* It is important because no one has said that the journey will be easy. The only way you will make it to the destination of your prize is if you can renew and replenish yourself so you hang in there and do not give up. In addition to working on the tasks at hand, you must keep your focus, stay energized, and remain determined. How can you do this if you are worn out, tired, and can't take it anymore? Honey, this is when I need a spa day . . . ! But seriously, take time to renew yourself. Even God took the seventh day off when God was creating the world. So why do you think you don't need time to rest as well?

THIS WEEK'S QUESTION TO PONDER IS: What are the ways in which you find renewal and restoration? If you don't have a plan in place, your mission is to identify what will bring you back to life when you grow weary and tired.

Come to me, all you that are weary and are carrying heavy burdens, and I will give you rest.
—MATTHEW 11:28

Peacefulness is an inner sense of calm—
it comes from becoming still—in order to reflect and
meditate on our inner wisdom and receive answers.
A peaceful heart is one that is free from worry and trouble.
It's becoming quiet so we can look at things quietly so we can
more clearly understand them and thus come up with
creative solutions. It is learning to live in the present.

—AUTHOR UNKNOWN

Sometimes the most urgent thing
you can possibly do is take a complete rest.

—ASHLEIGH BRILLIANT

Peace is not merely a distant goal that we seek
but a means by which we arrive at that goal.

—MARTIN LUTHER KING JR.

WEEK 13

Look out for the Po Po

On long trips, sometimes my father would drive faster than the speed limit. When he did, my dad would instruct my mom and me to "look out for the Po Po" (police). One of the habits I picked up from my father was driving fast. When I left home to attend college, which was only two hours away, my father told me, "The one thing you have to remember when you are on that highway is to look out for the Po Po so that you won't get a speeding ticket." My mother of course countered that with, "The reason speed limits are put into place is for safety. So there is no reason to rush. Take your time and enjoy your ride." Boy, do I take my mother's words to heed now. How does this apply to you where you are?

Well, as you drive on life's highway moving toward your prize, you must not rush. You must consciously drive the speed limit so that you don't have to worry about the Po Po. You see, if you take your time, you can actually enjoy the ride. Yes, this is a call to slow down. Savor the moment and smell the flowers instead of looking out for the good ole' Po Po!

Why should you slow down? You'll avoid those little things that happen to you when you rush to get things done quickly— like those impulse purchases that I always regret and end up returning to the store. Or how about when home builders build homes in a hurry. I have heard all kinds of stories where builders have forgotten or neglected to put important things in homes that ultimately causes structural fires or some other damage. The point I am trying to make is that "haste makes waste." So when you start to execute your plan toward your goal, your prize, you must not rush to complete it. Instead, take your time and do it right. For when you rush, you often leave out details, and sometimes it is the details that will make the difference in accomplishing your dream, your goal, your prize. "For there is still a vision for the appointed time; it speaks of the end, and does not lie. If it seems to tarry, wait for it; it will surely come, it will not delay." (Hab. 2:3).

Continuing to use Esther as an example, consider that Esther went through a year of preparation in order to have an opportunity to be considered for queen. It was not until after a year of preparation that Esther was even ready to be considered. At the appointed time, Esther became queen. Now, what if Esther had rushed and said, "this is ridiculous! It should not take this long to get ready to meet any man! Tell the king I want to meet him TODAY!" What do you think would have happened? I'll tell you what I think. Esther would have been bumped off the list and sent away. This moment as well as several others show how Esther had quiet patience and an understanding of timing.

Let's recall our earlier discussion during week 2—*Timing can sometimes be more important than the actual act itself.* Learning how to be graceful while waiting is key! Patience means gracefully smiling in the face of frustration and trusting that the time will come to make that move.

This is what I want you to remember as you travel toward your prize. Don't rush. Don't worry about looking out for the Po Po. Instead, take your time and stop to smell the roses along the way. This is the time for you to really appreciate the place you are in as you journey on your way. It is in the places between destinations that you learn the most. *Yes, the plan and the process are just as important as the destination.* It is the process that prepares you for the destination. Just think of Esther. If you rush, you will miss parts of the process needed to get to your destination.

Here's another example that may help. I would compare this to cooking a Thanksgiving turkey. If you take it out of the oven before the allocated time, it will not be done. If you turn up the temperature on the oven to rush the process, your turkey will browned quickly—so quickly that the outside may look done but the inside will be undone. You definitely want that turkey to be thoroughly cooked when you put it on the table. So, in the same vein, you too must take your time and enjoy the process of getting to your destination. This is definitely how preparation meets opportunity.

THIS WEEK, INSTEAD OF LOOKING OUT for the Po Po, focus on each step and smell the roses. Take time to appreciate and/or slow down and pay attention to what is going on around you. The question to ponder is: In what ways can you live in the present and learn to appreciate exactly where you are in the process of getting to your prize?

The plans of the diligent lead surely to abundance,
but everyone who is hasty comes only to want.
—PROVERBS 21:5

Fools rush in where angels fear to tread.
—ALEXANDER POPE

You won't realize the distance you've walked until
you take a look around and realize how far you've been.
—UNKNOWN

PART THREE

Don't Stay Stuck

WEEK 14

———

DON'T LOOK BACK

It is so easy in life to travel toward our future looking through the glasses of our past. This happens when we allow our past to hold us in the same place, thinking that everyone or everything will be just like what happened years ago. Or perhaps something that just happened this morning has stolen our joy. In this section of our "maximize moment," we must challenge ourselves to take off those glasses from the past, to not look back, and to make a different choice for ourselves: "You are not responsible for what has happened but for what you make of it."[8]

This is where we release any baggage—what someone did to you in the past that hurt you or hindered you, bad attitudes or habits that are holding you back, and so forth. It is when you let go of the past and be present in the today that you can really take hold of your journey! To stand in the present would mean the past does not control your life.

Let me share a story from the book of Genesis that may help explain this further. It is the story of Lot's wife, who could not resist looking back when she should have been looking only forward. This is when God was going to destroy the city of Sodom, but Lot, who had found favor with God, and Lot's family were to flee the city and thus be saved.

> When morning dawned, the angels urged Lot, saying, "Get up, take your wife and your two daughters who are here, or else you will be consumed in the punishment of the city." But he lingered; so the men seized him and his

wife and his two daughters by the hand, the Lord being merciful to him, and they brought him out and left him outside the city. When they had brought them outside, they said, "Flee for your life; do not look back or stop anywhere in the Plain; flee to the hills, or else you will be consumed. . . . Then the Lord rained on Sodom and Gomorrah sulphur and fire from the Lord out of heaven; and he overthrew those cities, and all the Plain, and all the inhabitants of the cities, and what grew on the ground. But Lot's wife, behind him, looked back, and she became a pillar of salt. (Gen. 19:15–26)

This is certainly a dramatic example, but the main point is that you have a choice. You have the choice to look forward and move toward your purpose or to look back and be hindered by your past. In essence, when you allow yourself to look back, you stay stuck in a holding pattern. How can you move forward while looking back? Think about it or stand up right now and try walking forward while looking behind you. If you are in a familiar room you might be able to do it, but when you are trying to move forward in a new place, your surroundings are not familiar. And if you look back while you move or drive forward, I guarantee you that you *will* run directly into something—that something that will hinder your forward progress.

This is definitely what I am talking about when I say *don't stay stuck*. If, like Lot's wife, you look back rather than focus on your goal, your future hopes and possibilities will be virtually impossible to achieve. For in looking back you stay stuck where you are and you never make it to where you can go. The overwhelming truth I hope you will learn is that "God wants to bring you through, to bring you out even better and to restore everything you have lost, plus give you more!"[9]

So what is holding you back? Is it something someone did to you or something someone said? Is it something that was done years ago or something that happened this morning that has hurt you or made you mad? Is it a bad relationship you are still not over? Is it coming to the realization that you are very much like your mother? Is it that woman who used to be your best friend and who is now a member of the "hateration club"? Does she talk about you behind your back and now has a grudge against you? Do you get angry every time you hear her name or see her face? Is it that relative whose death you are still grieving years later? Or are you still arguing with family members over their belongings? Or is never having had a relationship with your father causing you to have a bad relationship with men? Whatever it may be, this person, place, or thing has stolen your joy, and now it is time to take it back! Please don't think, "Oh none of these apply to me, so I am in no way stuck." We all have the propensity to be stuck or to get stuck.

THE FOCUS FOR THIS WEEK is to identify that one person, place, or thing that has the power to keep you stuck in one place. Over the next few weeks, as we continue to discuss how not to stay stuck, take time to write about it.

One day at a time—this is enough. Do not look back and grieve over the past, for it is gone; and do not be troubled about the future, for it has not yet come. Live in the present, and make it so beautiful it will be worth remembering.
—IDA SCOTT TAYLOR

The more anger toward the past you carry in your heart, the less capable you are of loving in the present.
—BARBARA DEANGELIS

WEEK 15

Did Ya Learn Something?

I hate to tell you this, but there is no way you will live on this earth and not go through something! You will make mistakes, get hurt, have sorrow, go through pain—basically you will have hard times. The goal in life is not to get away from hard times, but to learn something from them. So you can either stay stuck in the hurt, in the sorrow, or in making the same mistakes over and over—or you can *learn something from it.* What you can do with the pain and or mistakes of the past is to actually take the time to learn the lessons they teach you so that you can move forward.

If you open your eyes to what life teaches, you can become much wiser about people, places, things, and choices and how all these variables work together. It is the choices a person made that eventually hurt you, or the choice you made that eventually led to the mistake being made. Everything that occurs is based on choice. Yes, it IS as simple as your choice or someone else's choice. So, regardless of the situation, you must muster enough strength to realize that you cannot do anything about someone else's choice, but you can make your own choice to learn and move on! As tough as life's lessons can be, each holds within it insight that will make you a much better person if you take the time to look for the pathway to new growth. Here's an illustration.

You may have heard the biblical story of Joseph or you may have seen the musical *Joseph and the Amazing Technicolor Dreamcoat.* For those of you who haven't, I will give you a quick summary of it: Out of ten sons, Joseph was his father's favorite.

Joseph's brothers despised him for this and conspired to kill him. The two brothers who were assigned to kill Joseph could not go through with it and dropped Joseph into a dry well and left him to die. The brothers told their father that Joseph had been attacked by an animal and killed. What his brothers did not know was that Joseph had been found in the well by slave traders, who took him into Egypt and sold him to Potiphar, one of the Pharaoh's officers. To make a long story short, Joseph did not lose heart, and eventually the Pharaoh rewarded Joseph with the position of overseer of all Egypt. Joseph went from slave to second in command. Now that's what I call a blessing! This is a lesson on choosing not to stay stuck in one place, finding open windows when doors are shut, and staying positive through it all.

Many years later, a famine came. Guess where Joseph's brothers had to go to get food? Do you know that Bible verse that says God will make your enemies your footstool? Well, Joseph's brothers were at his feet having to beg for food. Yes, they had to go to the Pharaoh's right-hand man, Joseph, or they would die of starvation. Now, Joseph could have been bitter and evil and paid them back for all they had done to him, but instead he said to them, "Even though you intended to do harm to me, God intended it for good" (Gen. 50:20).

Joseph realized that all he went through was just so that he could be in a certain place at a certain time to save his family and the Hebrew people (the descendants of Joseph and his brothers became the twelve tribes of Israel). Yes, just like Esther, Joseph went through his tribulation "for such a time as this." If Joseph had stayed stuck in the hurt caused by his brothers, he would have never been able to be in the second greatest position in all of the land, the position that allowed him to save his entire family! Joseph's time-to-shine moment prepared him to meet that opportunity. What a powerful story!

In a lesson about life's hurts, Rick Warren puts it this way: "The way God is going to teach you the good qualities in life is to put you in the exact opposite situation. How will God teach you joy? By putting you in the middle of sorrow. How will God teach you love? By putting you around difficult people. How will God teach you peace? By putting you in the middle of chaos. God never wastes a hurt. He can bring good out of anything."[10] You see, the more difficult the situation or adversity, the more valuable the lessons learned. I have heard it put this way: life's adversities are God's universities. Therefore, in hard times or when facing adversity, you can choose to stay stuck—or to learn something. You can choose inner growth or inner turmoil. You can choose to look on the bright side or the dark side. *What will you choose?*

I AM SURE YOUR CHOICE is to not stay stuck or you would not be this far in our journey together. In this case, stop and think about what lessons you have learned about some of the things you have been through. You can write them down below or in your journal. The goal is to flip on the switch in this area and turn your pain into gratitude by focusing on the lesson and moving on from it, never to come back here again.

> *Adversity will surface in every life.*
> *How we meet it makes the difference.*
> —MARVIN J. ASHTON

> *When bad things happen in life, don't ask why. Ask how,*
> *and then discover what God wants to teach you.*
> —RICK WARREN

WEEK 16

—

PUSH on through to the Other Side

When you are going through something, do you ever stop long enough to think about what is on the other side? Staying focused on what you are going through rather than your goal can become the tie that binds you from moving beyond the current place to the other side. Now, I have never been pregnant or given birth, but I have been told that if women focused on the pain instead of focusing on the end result of all the pain—which is the baby that is to come—they wouldn't keep having babies! If you can stay focused on the baby, then you can endure the months of morning sickness and even the pain of childbirth because you know this is only for a moment and that your new baby boy or girl is on the other side of all this pain. So if it is possible to endure that kind of pain and focus on the baby, why can't you apply this same principle in your daily life? Why can't you stay focused on the destination, instead of the process you are going through to get there?

Now, this is not to say that pregnancy and birth are not beautiful—they are—and some women have an easier time than others. But there is no denying that the process involves a good deal of discomfort and then pain before it is over. It's just that the end result is worth it! If you stay focused on the negatives of pregnancy rather than on the baby, you can get stuck in what you are going through until you successfully give birth. You need to identify the difficulty, do what you can to get through it in the best way possible, and move forward.

Many relationships or situations in your life occur because an issue needs to be resolved. Let me give you an example. Perhaps you never knew your father, and now you have unsuccessful relationships with men. Don't get stuck in this recurring, painful process. Stop and realize what is happening. Why do you have negative relationships with men? You can't push past a problem if you can't identify the problem.

We may have know someone who, for whatever reason, falls in love with a "player," a man who cannot commit to one person—who leaves her for another woman. She might think that she has moved on, but then she attracts another man with the same "player" personality, who does the same thing. She must first realize what is happening, find out why she is repeating this pattern, before she can work past it. Get to know yourself intimately so that you can see what a problem is or why you are stuck and can't move forward.

Consider the employee who needs to be reprimanded or fired, but you, the boss, are too afraid to confront the employee. The employee finally quits and you hire someone else. To your surprise, the newly hired person is worse than your former employee. Do you get my point? You have hired the same type of person. It is time to do something about the ties in your life that bind you. Just as no woman would want to get stuck in prolonged labor, never to delivery the baby, you do not want to risk getting stuck in a tough spot in your life. Doing so can endanger yourself and your "baby"—your goal, your end result. You MUST go through the process of labor to get to the other side!

Whatever situation is holding you in a prolonged "pregnancy," it is time to go through the delivery, regardless of how hard it might be. No baby can transform from something inside you that may be hurting you into something beautiful until it has been born. You need to break the ties that are binding you. How do you do this? The first step is to recognize your issue, the second is to acknowledge it, and the third is to call it by name. So what is the tie that binds you? What situation do you just need to push out?

Being bound to a situation or circumstance can happen in many different ways. It can be in the form of abuse, dealing with an unfaithful partner, a mother or father who did not love you enough, being an adoptee and never fully resolving your feeling for your unknown birth family, the inability to speak up when you were a child, or even the pain of losing a job. I can go on. Whatever it is, stop now in this place and push it out! Recognize it for what it is—the tie that is binding you! It is the baby that must be birthed so that you can move on from these labor pains!

Yes, as long as we live on this earth, there is no way to get away from the pain. We go through things for a reason. If you can allow yourself to learn from the process, then you can be done with the pain and move on to the reward. You can actually receive the prize of holding your baby in your arms if you can learn when to push and when to breathe.

So in order to get to the other side, you must muster up the confidence and strength to carry the baby to full term and, when it is time, PUSH. Let go and move on and become the person you know you can be.

IN THE NEXT CHAPTER, we will discuss letting go. For now, the question to ponder is: What is holding you back from getting to the other side? What is that baby you are carrying? When will it be pushed out to become a beautiful part of your future?

Beloved, I do not consider that I have made it my own; but this one thing I do: forgetting what lies behind and straining forward to what lies ahead.
—PHILIPPIANS 3:13

Obstacles are things a person sees when he takes his eyes off his goal.
—E. JOSEPH COSSMAN

WEEK 17

Who Has Your Remote?

The first step in learning to let go is to figure out who or what has your remote. What do I mean by this? A remote is what controls the volume and/or the channels for a TV or other electronic item. To apply this concept when thinking about yourself, then what are you allowing to control you? To what or whom are you giving power in your life? What is able to change your channels?

According to stress management therapist Elizabeth Scott, "Research has shown that those with an internal locus of control—that is, they feel that they control their own destiny, rather than their fate being largely determined by external forces—tend to be happier, less depressed, and less stressed."[11] So in essence, Scott wants you to take full control of yourself and not allow your mood to shift according to the people, places, or things around you.

If while driving to work another driver cuts you off, would you allow that person to steal your joy? Are you a person who yells at the driver in the other car even after you can no longer see the other car? In that moment, the other driver has your remote control. You have allowed that driver to take what may have been a peaceful morning and turn you into a state of angry rage. Believe it or not, your reaction to that driver is based on the choices you make. You can choose to be or not to be angry. This is a simple example, but things can happen that may definitely turn your sunshine into rain if you allow it—if you allow another to control your remote. It is important for you to identify to whom or to what you give your remote control, what you allow to affect you. Just what has your remote? If it is not in your hands, it's time to *take back your remote!*

How do you take back your remote? First, you must realize that in any given situation you have the choice to decide how you will react. You can't change how other people act or react but you can definitely change how you allow their actions to affect you. Yes, you can choose how you counteract or you can even change the role this person, place, or thing has in your life so that it cannot affect you. If this is something that you can't get away from, then what you need to do is figure out who you need to be in that moment so that *you* have your remote instead of whatever it is taking your remote and flipping your channel. You can decide to smile when you are cut off in traffic and move on. On the other hand, you can stay stuck and angry at that other driver long after he or she is gone.

The most important thing you can do to take back the remote in your life is to first take notice of how things affect you. If you feel yourself being negative, you have to choose to flip that remote to the positive channel. Phrases like "I can't" should be released from your vocabulary. Instead, figure out what you *can* do. Instead of fighting "what is," you need to learn to accept and to be at peace.

Remember, you can't control most other people or things. But you can control how you interact with or react to them. By choosing to have peace, and trusting that what is meant to be shall be, you can hold onto a positive outlook in all things that come your way. By choosing what you allow to control you, you actually allow more positive energy to flow to you instead of trying to force what may not be meant to be; if it doesn't fit, don't force it.

You have to be determined to accept people, places, and things as they are and to know that you can't change people. All you can do is change *you.* You thus can change how something or someone affects you. By doing this, you are taking back your remote. You have the power in your hands to release the hold that negative emotions, people, places, and/or things have had on you. You can reclaim your power and give yourself the gift of peace of mind. You can move into a positive direction toward your dream.

THIS WEEK, IDENTIFY WHAT IS HOLDING YOU BACK. Then answer: To what and to whom do you give your remote? What or who steals your joy? What or who can make a good day turn into a bad one?

You cannot control what happens to you, but you can control your attitude toward what happens to you, and in that, you will be mastering change rather than allowing it to master you.

—BRIAN TRACY

In essence, if we want to direct our lives, we must take control of our consistent actions. It's not what we do once in a while that shapes our lives, but what we do consistently.

—ANTHONY ROBBINS

The best years of your life are the ones in which you decide your problems are your own. You do not blame them on your mother, the ecology, or the president. You realize that you control your own destiny.

—ALBERT ELLIS

The secret of success is learning how to use pain and pleasure instead of having pain and pleasure use you. If you do that you're in control of your life. If you don't, life controls you.

—ANTHONY ROBBINS

This life is yours. Take the power to choose what you want to do and do it well. Take the power to love what you want in life and love it honestly. Take the power to control your own life. No one else can do it for you. Take the power to make your life happy.

—SUSAN POLIS SCHUTZ

WEEK 18

I Forgive You

The next step you must master in learning to let go is forgiveness. Yes, every one of us has been through something that has hurt us and has left us with feelings of anger, bitterness, and maybe even revenge. To forgive is the ability to let go of those feelings. It is to release any negative thoughts that are currently attached to the person who has hurt you, talked about you, or somehow just done you wrong.

You may think to yourself, I have no problem letting go of the person, but yet you continue to hold a grudge. Holding grudges is *not* letting go! According to Webster's dictionary, "a grudge is a feeling of deep-seated resentment or ill will." Holding a grudge means you are still carrying with you or holding on to feelings from that person or thing that hurt you or made you angry. In other words, you have not truly forgiven the person, and this lack of forgiveness is what leads you to bitterness. To move past this, you must get rid of this burden and let go of the anger, hurt, animosity, hostility, and resentment. Another thing: to let go is not simply "to forget" or "to ignore."

By all means, you should carry with you the lessons you have learned from what happened. However, *you need to release the emotional baggage that is tied to the event that you are carrying around with you.* If you don't let it go, you will carry it into the next relationship, job, or similar situation.

So I am calling you to learn the lessons you need to release yourself from the negative emotions tied to the hurtful past. You must do this so that you will not stay stuck in a negative pattern. To move into your promise, your purpose, your destiny, and your dreams, you must release and forgive so that you can be open to and present for new opportunities.

What is forgiveness? . . .

Forgiveness is for you, not the offender. Forgiveness is taking back your power. Forgiveness is taking responsibility for how you feel. Forgiveness is about your healing and not about the people who hurt you. . . . Forgiveness helps you get control over your feelings. Forgiveness can improve your mental and physical health. Forgiveness is a choice. . . .

What forgiveness is not:

Forgiveness is not condoning unkindness. Forgiveness is not forgetting that something painful happened. Forgiveness is not excusing poor behavior. . . . Forgiveness is not denying or minimizing your hurt. Forgiveness does not mean reconciling with the offender.[12]

I am sure you are thinking, Nicole, these people did me wrong and I need to pay them back! "Beloved, never avenge yourselves, but leave room for the wrath of God; for it is written, 'Vengeance is mine, I will repay,' says the LORD" (Rom. 12:19).

I had to share that with you because when I truly learned to let go and let God, I saw how God can repay wrong better than you or I could ever have repaid the other person! However, the trick here is to not wish for evil on that person, but to give thought to this person and how he or she affected you and to actually learn to pray for the person. Scripture says, "No, 'if your enemies are hungry, feed them; if they are thirsty, give them something to drink; for by doing this you will heap burning coals on their heads.' Do not be overcome by evil, but overcome evil with good." (Rom. 12:20–21).

I did not understand the coals of fire part so I looked it up and found this proverb: "For you will heap coals of fire on their heads, and the Lord will reward you" (Prov. 25:22).

My take-away is that when you repay evil with good, God will truly bless you for doing what is right, especially when it is hard to do. Yes, forgiving and letting go can be very hard things to do, but it's even harder and more stressful to hold on to grudges. It takes more energy to be negative than to be positive. Plus it just feels so doggone good to be positive. Forgiveness is a powerful tool toward change.

To forgive definitely frees you from the burden of yesterday so that you can pursue your tomorrows. Tim Laurence, founder of the Hoffman Institute, said, "I have seen people whose lives have been determined by a grievance that has affected not only themselves, but also generations after them. To then see that person forgive and be able to move on in their lives is like watching them unlocking the door to their own prison and stepping out into freedom."[13] I like to put it this way: It is like a caterpillar becoming a butterfly. If you visualize that statement, I am sure you can see the difference in the two. Or maybe it is not someone else or something you need to forgive; maybe you need to forgive *yourself.* Maya Angelou said this about self-forgiveness:

> I don't know if I continue, even today, always liking myself. But what I learned to do many years ago was to forgive myself. It is very important for every human being to forgive herself or himself because if you live, you will make mistakes—it is inevitable. But once you do and you see the mistake, then you forgive yourself and say, "Well, if I'd known better I'd have done better," that's all. So you say to people whom you think you may have injured, "I'm sorry," and then you say to yourself, "I'm sorry." If we all hold on to the mistake, we can't see our own glory in the mirror because we have the mistake between our faces and the mirror; we can't see what we're capable of being. You can ask forgiveness of others, but in the end the real forgiveness is in one's own self. I think that young men

and women are so caught by the way they see themselves. Now mind you. When a larger society sees them as unattractive, as threats, as too black or too white or too poor or too fat or too thin or too sexual or too asexual, that's rough. But you can overcome that. The real difficulty is to overcome how you think about yourself. If we don't have that we never grow, we never learn, and sure as hell we should never teach.[14]

The act of forgiveness is a decision; it is a decision not to allow this person, place, or thing to continue to add stress and negativity to your life. It is a decision to take back your remote and to take over the control of your own feelings. Whatever it is, whether you or someone or something else, each of us must identify who or what is holding us back. What is keeping you down? What is making you think of who you used to be and not ready to see you do better? Who are you still mad at for something done years ago? What grudge are you holding that keeps you in a place of bitterness and resentment? Now is your moment to step into your freedom and forgive!

WITH THAT SAID, whom do you need to forgive? What do you need to let go of so that you open your life up to possibility and promise? Write it down here or in your journal.

When you hold resentment toward another,
you are bound to that person or condition by an emotional
link that is stronger than steel. Forgiveness is the only way
to dissolve that link and get free.

—CATHERINE PONDER

Hanging onto resentment is letting someone
you despise live rent-free in your head.

—ANN LANDERS

Forgiveness does not change the past,
but it does enlarge the future.

—PAUL BOESE

Any fool can criticize, condemn, and complain,
but it takes character and self-control to be
understanding and forgiving.

—DALE CARNEGIE

WEEK 19

REHEARSE IT OR RELEASE IT

Our topic this week is all about the decision between staying stuck or letting go. This is really simple: either you *rehearse it or release it.* You can either repeat the same scene in your life by allowing those things that have hurt you or have hindered you to happen over and over again, or you can let them go and be free from them so that you can push past toward building the life of your dreams.

So what is the difference between rehearsing and releasing? Well, when you think of rehearse, what do you think of? I think of doing something over and over again. A great example of this is what we talked about a few weeks ago. The children of Israel turned an eleven-day journey into a forty-year trip as they rehearsed the same day over and over again. Their negative outlook and disbelief kept them going around and around that same mountain again and again. They could not allow themselves to see past where they were so their faith could take them where they belonged. They kept living through the things that had happened in the past. This is absolutely what you do when you allow things that have occurred in your life to play over and over again. If you want to move forward in your life and not stay stuck, you must make a different choice—to release whatever is holding you back—*by letting it go.*

Some unknown author on ThinkExist.com has said, "Getting over a painful experience is much like crossing monkey bars. You have to let go at some point in order to move forward."

To release or to let go is an act of surrender. Let me put it this way, have you ever heard the saying: "Let go and let God?" Well, imagine that God is in the driver's seat of your car and you are in the back seat. Would you trust that God knew the direction you are headed in? Or would you be a backseat driver, yelling out where to turn and which way to go and complaining that it was taking too long? If you said to yourself that you would sit in the back and trust the direction you are headed, then you have surrendered.

According to the Webster's dictionary, surrender is to give (oneself) up into the power of another, to relinquish. So if you look at surrender from this context, then you realize that you cannot control how people act and the decisions that they make. Instead of fighting "what is," you must learn to accept and to be at peace. You must relinquish or release the need to be in control of everything and, in essence, to realize that God is in control! "Trust in the Lord with all your heart, and do not rely on your own insight" (Prov. 3:5).

So instead of always asking, "Why did this happen?" "Why would they do that?" learn to trust that "[w]e know that all things work together for good for those who love God, who are called according to [God's] purpose" (Rom. 8:28).

Beginning in our next chapter, we will discuss faith. If you can trust that all things work together for the good and realize that all you *can* control is how you allow things or people to affect you and/or how you choose to interact or react to them, then you can have peace. By choosing to have peace, and trusting that what is meant to be shall be, you can hold on to more of a positive outlook on all things that come your way. To keep yourself in this positive space, you must rid yourself of all negative people, emotions, and thoughts that haunt you and take up space and steal your joy.

These things infiltrate your being and affect how you relate to people, places, and things that are currently in your life as well as those to come. By letting go, you actually allow more positive energy to flow instead of trying to force what may not be meant to be. If it doesn't fit, don't force it.

Letting go means to release and to take back your remote, to forgive anyone or anything that has hurt you or offended you. By forgiving, releasing, and letting go, you are by no means acting like your feelings of hurt, anger, and/or hatred are not there. There is no way you can get rid of the circumstances that have made you feel the way you do. Instead, what you are doing is choosing to no longer allow them to affect you. You are letting go of what these feelings do to you. You are moving away from the notion of staying stuck and dwelling on the situation. You are accepting what has happened and moving on. To sum up our last two weeks, you should be able to answer these two questions: Have you taken back your remote or not? Have you freed yourself to forgive?

THE QUESTION THIS WEEK IS: On the monkey bars of life, what is it that you need to let go of in order to take hold of possibility in your life?

Breathe. Let go. And remind yourself that this very moment is the only one you know you have for sure.
—OPRAH WINFREY

Let go. Why do you cling to pain? There is nothing you can do about the wrongs of yesterday. It is not yours to judge. Why hold on to the very thing which keeps you from hope and love?
—LEO BUSCAGLIA

WEEK 20

Rise above It

Now that we have discussed how to deal with and resolve whatever has emotionally bound us, the next step is learning to live in a mode where nothing will bind us ever again. We do this by learning to *rise above it*. Rise above situations and circumstances that will try to remind you of what happened in the past, that make you feel or think negatively about where you currently are, or that come just to plain old mess up your day! Rising above is learning to hold your head up high and not allow anything or anyone to steal your joy.

"My brothers and sisters, whenever you face trials of any kind, consider it nothing but joy" (James 1:2). James, the brother of Jesus, talks about how we are to deal with trials. Instead of thinking of them as terrible things, we are to consider our trials as nothing but joy. So you must take your focus off the storm and focus on the rainbow that will come after it. Know that joy will come when you rise above the current circumstance and do not allow it or anyone to steal your joy. You have to keep a positive outlook and smile in the face of fear. This is definitely a very easy way to connect to the character of Esther, whom you are following in your journey throughout the book.

You see, Esther is a great example of someone who knew how to rise above it. She was able to rise above being an orphan to become queen. She was able to rise above the fact that her husband was preparing to kill all of her people. Instead Esther focused on what she needed to do to save her people—she looked for that rainbow—and that is how she was able to come to her time-to-shine moment. Another example is Joseph, whom I discussed in week 15. Joseph also was able to rise above his circumstance, because, despite all that he went through, he kept a positive attitude. When it was all said and done he was able to say, "God intended it for good, in order to preserve a numerous people, as he is doing today" (Gen. 50:20).

Joseph realized that all he went through was just so that he could be in this place at this time to save his family, his people. If Joseph did not rise above every negative thing that came his way, he would have never made it to that moment. So what does this all mean? Well, it is like when you hear so-and-so talking about you. Instead of trying to get back at that person or being mean when you see that person—rolling your eyes and other negative body language—you must rise above it.

As you do, realize that this is that person's issue and not yours. Keep your head up, smile, put those shoulders back, and rise above it. You do that by keeping a positive demeanor. There is no way that you will allow a hater to make you stoop down to his or her level, right? Or as I like to say, no one is going to make me mess up my ticket to heaven. Or how about when you find out your man is cheating on you and he breaks up with you? This is not the time for you to cry and roll on the floor. It is time for you to realize that *you* are a gift and that *he* messed up his blessing as you dust your shoulder off to *rise above it*. You have got to know that he did not deserve you if this is how he treated you. Another man who *will* appreciate who you are will find you!

So the key is to learn how to rise above where you currently are in order to partake in where you can go. The ultimate destination of your prize can only be found learning how to not allow the negative to touch you but to live in a positive place. Rise above it!

Did your mother or grandmother ever tell you when you were little to keep your head up? Why do you think when you are going through something people will tell you to keep your head up? When you are not feeling good about yourself you might say, "I am feeling down." Well, it is time to challenge yourself to look up and rise above what *is* to what *can be* if you can choose to rise above it!

It is time for each of us to learn who we are, and once we know who we are, we will then realize that we are not competing with anyone else. The man for you will have eyes only for you. Your true friends will not be haters.

YES, GIRL, YOU ARE THE BEST! So rise above it! Rise to the occasion. Rise up and marvel in who you are! Next week we will explore what it means to rise above it. For now, think about and write out the ways you can rise above situations and circumstances to arrive at the destination of your dreams.

*I know it seems hard sometimes, but remember
one thing, through every dark night, there's a bright day after
that. So no matter how hard it gets, keep your chest out,
keep your head up, and handle it.*
—TUPAC

*When love is lost, do not bow your head in sadness;
instead keep your head up high and gaze at the stars, for that
is where your broken heart has been sent to heal!*
—UNKNOWN

Happiness is not a destination in which you arrive;
it is your journey there.

—UNKNOWN

Little minds are tamed and subdued by misfortune;
but great minds rise above them.

—WASHINGTON IRVING

WEEK 21

BE AN EAGLE

Last week I talked about rising above whatever is holding you back. I'm calling you to challenge yourself to spread your wings and rise above like an eagle rises above the earth when it soars. I am calling you to be an eagle! When I think of an eagle, I think of a bird that surpasses all others. An eagle can fly to tremendous heights. Webster's dictionary describes an eagle as "a bird noted for its strength, size, keenness of vision, and powers of flight." When I think of eagles, I also think of this Bible verse: "But those who wait for the Lord shall renew their strength, they shall mount up with wings like eagles, they shall run and not be weary, they shall walk and not faint" (Isa. 40:31).

So if those who wait on God will mount up on wings like eagles, then if you can focus on God and not what you may be going through, it means you can mount up with wings like eagles and soar above it. When you can keep a positive attitude through it all, you are soaring on wings like eagles. If you can trust that all that you are going through is for a purpose, then you can be an eagle and soar to great heights. If you are an eagle, even when you are not going through something, you are not allowing the lower flying birds to get to you as you fly to greater heights. Translation: when the haters hate on you, you don't allow it to affect you. You rise above it and hold your head up high. If you are an eagle, you *soar*. You ascend to a higher level. Your attitude depicts your altitude, so the more positive you are, the higher the altitude. You are operating on a more exalted level. Staying in a negative place or allowing yourself to have a negative demeanor or attitude just keeps you on the ground. You are not able to soar to great heights or to really fly at all—let alone fly as high as you possibly can.

Being negative also means you are that crab in the barrel (you know that old saying) and you are keeping yourself down never to rise above! But if you are an eagle, you have keenness of vision. You are keeping your eyes on the prize and not allowing the storms that come to blow you off your path. Keenness of vision allows you to tap into that inner urge (which is God's voice whispering to you) to know when a storm is coming so that you can put on your holy armor and be ready to withstand it.

You see, an eagle allows the storm to become the wind beneath its wings rather than a force to fight against, as the lessons learned from every storm take you just that much higher. An eagle is strong, determined, focused, confident, unwavering, steadfast, and tenacious. An eagle definitely knows and dwells in her power . . . do I need to go on? This description by an unknown author that has been making the rounds of Internet blogs for more than a decade illustrates my point perfectly:

SOAR LIKE AN EAGLE

Did you know that an eagle knows when a storm is approaching long before it breaks? The eagle will fly to some high spot and wait for the winds to come. When the storm hits, it sets its wings so that the wind will pick it up and lift it above the storm. While the storm rages below, the eagle is soaring above it.

The eagle does not escape the storm. It simply uses the storm to lift it higher. It rises on the winds that bring the storm. When the storms of life come upon us—and all of us will experience them—we can rise above them by setting our minds and our belief toward God. The storms do not have to overcome us. We can allow God's power to lift us above them.

God enables us to ride the winds of the storm that bring sickness, tragedy, failure, and disappointment in our lives. We can soar above the storm. Remember, if we are really honest to ourselves, it is not the burdens of life that weigh us down, it is how we handle them.[15]

It's time for each of us to learn how to be an eagle and rise above negative situations, circumstances, people, places, and things so that all the positive forces in our lives will define our altitude and allow us to fly to ever greater heights. As we become like an eagle, we are able to stay focused on becoming the person that God has ordained each of us to become.

IN THE LAST WEEK OR MONTH, what was one event that you know you should have let go and risen above? In what ways would you act differently if you could do it all over again?

WEEK 22

———

WHAT IS GROWING ON YOUR TREE?

So why all of the talk over the past weeks about staying stuck? Well, it all boils down to what you produce in your life, which is essentially what you are growing on your tree. When I talked about rehearse or release, letting go, who has your remote, forgiveness, rising above it, and being an eagle, I was exploring things that should be nurtured, or watered, in your life. What you water is what will grow. Let me use this Bible verse to help illustrate what I mean:

> You will know them by their fruits. Are grapes gathered from thorns, or figs from thistles? In the same way, every good tree bears good fruit, but the bad tree bears bad fruit. A good tree cannot bear bad fruit, nor can a bad tree bear good fruit. Every tree that does not bear good fruit is cut down and thrown into the fire. Thus you will know them by their fruits. (Matt. 7:16–20)

So what fruit is growing on your tree? What are you producing in your life? Understand that whatever is manifesting in your life is in direct correlation with what you are focusing on or allowing to be produced in your life. The words we speak. The people we have around us. The actions we take. Everything has to do with what is produced in your life. Therefore, if all that is around you and inside of you—by way of your thoughts—is in alignment with your desires, then you will be in line with the woman you wish to become.

If you look at yourself as a tree, the most direct connection to a tree would be your heart. Whatever is in our heart is what is manifested in your life. So, what is in your heart? Is it bitterness, resentment? If it is, what do you think that produces in your life? Or do you have hope and love in your heart? If so, what do you think that produces in your life? Over the past weeks, we have really talked about pruning the bad fruit, just using different language and other metaphors—the resentment, bitterness, hurt, anger, pain, sadness. You must uproot weeds and plant love, self-confidence, harmony, happiness, and so on. I repeat, whatever is planted in your heart is what will manifest in your life.

Remember this verse from week 7: "As a [wo]man thinks in [her] heart, so is [s]he." (Prov. 23:7 NKJV). Do you speak positive or negative words about yourself? Do you have people in your life who are positive or negative influences? Do your friends and family believe in you and/or your dreams? If any of your responses pertain to the negative, what will you do to change it? The whole point is that you should only want people and things in your life that will help you grow positive fruit. This is the byproduct that you want to produce in your life. Yes, when you don't feel very positive or when you are going through something, it is not easy to be positive. However, if you can make a daily choice to stay positive, your tree of life will produce good fruit. Therefore, on those bad days when you are going through a hard time, you must choose to remain positive despite the outlook or how you feel in that moment.

"We are afflicted in every way, but not crushed; perplexed, but not driven to despair; persecuted, but not forsaken; struck down, but not destroyed" (2 Cor. 4:8–9). During difficulty in my life, the only way I can remain positive is to focus on God, which is focusing on my faith. When I am hard pressed with issue after issue, I can smile in the face of adversity just like Ms. Esther and have a quiet assurance and know, despite what my current situation looks like, that, "all things work together for good" (Rom. 8:28).

Remember Joseph? He too modeled, through extremely difficult circumstances, that the key to finding the rainbow after the storm is to remain positive. I know for me the *greatest* ingredient of this positive disposition is really learning how to find light in a dark place. The light always leads me to focus on my faith. Yes, this is when I call on God! Even in calling on the Almighty, just think if you had been beaten, forced to carry a cross, endured being spat on, talked about, and lied about. Would you be able to remain positive and focus on how all things work together for the good? Jesus did, and he is the ultimate example of rising above it all! His journey was definitely for a purpose. Whew! Jesus is definitely on a level of positivity that I aspire to. I guess that's what that popular slogan, "What would Jesus do?" means. Jesus was so positive. He is our model on how not to stay stuck, how to rise above to become the person God has called each of us to be.

THINK ABOUT IT—in any given situation, how might you flip your reaction and think about what Jesus would do? Write your answer(s) here or in your journal.

Each day comes bearing its own gifts.
Untie the ribbons.

—RUTH ANN SCHABACKER

Dwell upon the brightest parts in every prospect . . .
and strive to be pleased with the present circumstances.

—ABRAM TUCKER

Trouble is only opportunity in work clothes.

—HENRY J. KAISER

God brings men into deep waters not
to drown them, but to cleanse them.

—JOHN H. AUGHEY

Sorrow looks back, worry looks around, faith looks up.

—GUIDEPOSTS

PART FOUR

Know God Intimately

WEEK 23

Our First Date

As we begin to explore this thing called faith, we begin by looking at getting to know someone intimately, which is the basis for a great relationship. To explore this we will use that old tried and true first point of contact, which for most would be a first date. You know how we do it: we put on our best self, trying to get to know the other person. We ask questions to really try to figure out who that person is. So when we are looking at developing our own personal relationship with God, this is indeed the same place we start. But let's take a step back. You may be asking, why do I even need a personal relationship with God in the first place? Let me start at a point that will easily transition us from our previous principle—don't stay stuck—into this one:

> Therefore take up the whole armor of God, so that you may be able to withstand on that evil day, and having done everything, to stand firm. Stand therefore, and fasten the belt of truth around your waist, and put on the breastplate of righteousness. As shoes for your feet put on whatever will make you ready to proclaim the gospel of peace. With all of these, take the shield of faith, with which you will be able to quench all the flaming arrows of the evil one. Take the helmet of salvation, and the sword of the Spirit, which is the word of God. Pray in the Spirit at all times in every prayer and supplication. To that

end keep alert and always persevere in supplication for all the saints. (Eph. 6:13–18)

We each have our very own piece of God's armor, which was tailor-made just for us. In order for it to be effective, however, you have to put it on. Putting it on will help you fight against those things that try to keep you stuck. Wearing God's armor is what you do when you establish a relationship with God. So to put on the full armor or to embark on this relationship or to initiate the "first date" in your relationship with God—what better way to do this than by hearing the stories others have told about God's magnificent powers? You know, before or right after the first date, you ask folks all about the guy you just went out with! Why not take this same approach and get to know more about God? Stop listening to others' stories. Find out for yourself about God and what God has done.

Let me share a personal story. In 1994, I set out on a journey to get to know Nicole. I was going to date no one but me! After one too many bad break-ups, I figured it was time for me to stop trying to find a man and to actually find *Nicole*! At first, it was really weird. I took myself to dinner at a restaurant—yes, dinner alone. I must say it felt like everyone was staring at me. After I got over my fear of eating alone, in time (you see I did this a few times) I began to enjoy being with just me. It was during this period when I first discovered God inside of me.

No, I mean I *really* discovered God. Yes, I had gone to church for as long as I can remember, but before that moment in 1994, I was having a relationship with God through my mother. I remember my pastor saying, "ya know, friends don't fly free," and I think that kicked it in for me. This meant that it was time for me to seek my own personal relationship with God instead of having a relationship with God through my mother's faith. So what I share with you is based on my own experiences. No, I am not a preacher, but I am a woman who has seen how having a relationship with God has transformed my own life. It has changed how I treat people and talk to people. It has changed my viewpoint on life and really has changed me from a negative person to a positive person. (Can you believe that I used to be negative?!) Well, God really can be a trusted friend and an advisor. God's best advice, as the seasoned elders would say, is "right in the good book!"

It is amazing to me how easy it is to get to know God just by exploring the Bible. In 1994, reading God's word was exactly what jump-started my wonderful new friendship with God. You know, I sure wish I had a book on some of the men I dated before I met my husband. Honey, I should not have even given them the time of day. So, as you begin dating God—yes, I said dating God—explore, meaning that you are now really getting to know God as you would a person on a first date. Even if you feel like you already have a relationship, it never hurts to renew your connection. Let's examine this relationship concept together as we begin to communicate with God and look at what scripture says about God.

Exploring this relationship with God has given me the strength to stand up against the things in my past that tried to hold me back, forming who I used to be. Then I learned to "put on the whole armor of God, . . . to stand against the wiles of the devil" (Eph. 6:11).

It is the holy armor that keeps me safe when I am being attacked by a hater, so I can stay focused on my own purpose and the promises of God. It is the holy armor that gives me peace when chaos happens all around me. It helps me to stay clear and see beyond my current storm to the rainbow ahead. So I no longer run from problems or hard situations; instead, I run to God, knowing that all things work together for the good.

Today, some twenty years after I got to know God for myself, I can definitely call God my homey as I walk and talk and hang out with God every day!

SO THIS WEEK, I encourage you to explore and begin to get to know or renew your relationship with God. Each morning, I start my day reading a daily devotional. I read *Our Daily Bread.* It helps me to grow in God. The following space is available for you to write the ways in which you will explore getting to know God or learning to know God on a deeper level.

Faith is like radar that sees through the fog—the reality
of things at a distance that the human eye cannot see.
—CORRIE TEN BOOM

Faith sees the invisible, believes the incredible,
and receives the impossible.
—ANONYMOUS

Without faith, nothing is possible.
With it, nothing is impossible.
—MARY MCLEOD BETHUNE

Faith is taking the first step even when
you don't see the whole staircase.
—MARTIN LUTHER KING JR.

Faith is a living, daring confidence in God's grace,
so sure and certain that a man could stake his life
on it a thousand times.
—MARTIN LUTHER KING JR.

WEEK 24

—

SHHH . . . DID YOU HEAR THAT?

Let's continue the conversation from last week about getting to know someone. When you begin to know someone, you must learn to listen. We have all heard how relationships have ended because one of the individuals in the relationship did not feel heard. Thousands of relationships end because of one thing—an inability to listen. Consider those who end up being in a relationship with someone only to realize later that they barely knew the person. Well, the basis of this lack of knowledge is because at some point, someone did not listen to the other. Someone did not really listen to what the person was saying, not only in words but in the other person's actions. Maybe those actions did not mirror what the person was saying. As Oprah has said, "When people show you who they are, believe them."

In any relationship, listening is key. Shhh. Did you hear that? It amazes me how often when we get an inner feeling about someone we ignore it. So listen not just with your ears, but with your heart. Listen to that other person's heart, for out of the heart, actions speak.

To listen involves two things: hearing and understanding. *Hearing* is what we focused on last week. To hear is to take in and/or grasp what other people are saying, doing, and being. It is knowing what they mean by the words they speak. And all of their actions and deeds are actually their words made flesh.

This week we'll talk about *understanding*. This is when you take what you have heard and you really figure out what it means, who this person really is. When you understand how someone thinks, then you can understand the way he or she ticks. You will gain insight as to why people do what they do. Why is this so important? Well, let's go a little deeper and look at the two parts of this word "understand."

"Under"—when I think of "under," I think of looking beyond what is on the surface, digging down beneath the covering. "Stand"—when I think of "stand," I think of holding or maintaining a certain position.

So the two words together might mean that we need to look beyond the surface to see a person's stance in life, which comes out of the heart. And out of the heart come all of one's innermost values. So understanding is looking beyond the surface to truly comprehend why a person thinks and acts as he or she does. In looking this deeply, you can begin to understand a person. You must seek this clarity, so that you are clear on who this person is and how he or she thinks, moves, and has being. Listen to your heart. Explore the words and thoughts that come out of the person. Listening is an active process where you take all of the information that comes your way and explore what it all means in relation to the person.

This need to listen is critical also to building your relationship with God. It is in hearing story after story, sermon after sermon, that you will grow in faith. It is in digging deeper to really understand how God works, how God moves, and what God's being is all about that you will begin to form a true relationship. As you discover God by digging deeper to explore who God is, you will form your own relationship with the Almighty.

It is in this place of relationship that our theme character for the year, Ms. Esther, found herself. You see, when Esther heard the news that her husband's right-hand man wanted to kill all of the Jews, her people, she fasted and prayed for three days. She fasted and prayed. She waited to hear from God about what to do. She knew she needed to sit still in the presence of God, based on what God had done in her life in the past. Esther knew this based on her already having built a relationship with the Almighty.

Now, we each are from various backgrounds, ages, and stages in life, and each of our life experiences differ; so my relationship with God will not be the same as your relationship. My testimonies will differ from yours as we each build a base of our own faith, our own relationship. It is your life experiences that have made you who you are. It is this space of difference that lets each of us have our own special relationship with God. It is seeking God for ourselves and looking at God through our own lenses that will allow us to understand God for ourselves and begin to understand how to focus on faith. So as you explore who God is for yourself, shhh. Listen. Stop and ask yourself, "Did you hear that?"

THIS WEEK, for our time to ponder and reflect, sit in a quiet place and just listen to God speak to your soul.

*We look upon prayer as a means of getting things
for ourselves; the Bible's idea of prayer is that we may
get to know God Himself.*

—OSWALD CHAMBERS

*Listening is a magnetic and strange thing—
a creative force. When we really listen to people there
is an alternating current, and this recharges us so that
we never get tired of each other.
We are constantly being re-created.*

—BRENDA UELAND

Listen and attend with the ear of your heart.

—SAINT BENEDICT

*The most basic of all human needs is the need
to understand and to be understood. The best way to
understand people is to listen to them.*

—RALPH NICHOLAS

WEEK 25

THINGS THAT MAKE YOU GO, HMM . . .

Do you remember the Arsenio Hall show that came on in the 1990s? Well, one of my favorite segments on his show was called, "Things That Make You Go, Hmm." Arsenio would share various current events, or ponder things done by certain people, share places or things that were happening in the world as a moment of contemplation and reflection. Of course this moment had a funny spin to it! However, when I think back to this segment, it really makes me contemplate many things, and it makes me curious about what the word "contemplate" really means.

So in my curiosity, I looked up its definition and was surprised at what I found. According to Webster's, contemplation is "a concentration on spiritual things as a form of private devotion, a state of mystical awareness of God's being, an act of considering with attention or the act of regarding steadily." Wow, I never expected to see that definition! So if I apply what Arsenio meant into knowing God intimately, this really does bring us to an awareness of who God is with our limited human understanding. The psalmist said, "I will meditate on your precepts, and contemplate your ways" (Psa. 119:15 NKJV).

It is in this place of contemplation that you begin to think about, reflect on, and apply the various things you find out about God. This will influence how you think and ultimately what comes out of your heart. You may ask, "Why is this important?" By contemplating God's works, ways, purposes, and promises, you get to know who God is and what God has done, which then develops into a relationship between you and God. It is similar to getting to know someone—the more you get to know a person and spend time with that person, the more the relationship grows between the two of you.

Developing a relationship? I know that the more I get to know God, the more I marvel at God's works, and the more I want to learn and become a woman after God's own heart. This is more than a call to religion. It is a call to a relationship. You see, standing in a garage does not make me a car any more than my going to church makes me a Christian. I need to go to church so that I can learn more about God and fellowship with others who are on my same journey. But a relationship is far more than religion—it is getting to know God for *yourself.* And to do so, you definitely need these three ingredients: communication, concentration, and contemplation. You need these three "Cs" to know, understand, and meditate on who God is. Therefore, as I grow in God and begin to know God for myself, I can adopt the Apostle Paul's advice: "Put these things into practice, devote yourself to them, so that all may see your progress (1 Tim. 4:15).

As I began to meditate more and more on God, I realized that my attitude began to change for the better. My friends, who knew me back in the day, knew me to have a pretty bad attitude. God has turned my attitude into something much more pleasant as I seek peace every day of my life. How is it, you may ask, that the more I get to know God, the more I want to be like God? As I began to know God, I lived by this scripture passage: "Do not be conformed to this world, but be transformed by the renewing of your minds, so that you may discern what is the will of God— what is good and acceptable and perfect (Rom. 12:2).

I found that as I contemplated on all that I was learning, I was becoming a better *me!* I learned how to treat people better and how to not let little things steal my joy. Some days I am better at it than others, but now I have a tool that helps me smile and find a rainbow in every storm. I must admit that, for a woman who had absolutely no patience, the thing I am still working on is found in Philippians 4: "Do not worry about anything, but in everything by prayer and supplication with thanksgiving let your requests be made known to God. And the peace of God, which surpasses all understanding, will guard your hearts and your minds in Christ Jesus" (Phil. 4:6–7).

What do I mean by all of this is? Well as you take a moment to think on all these things that definitely make you go, "Hmm …," you begin to dig in and explore your curiosity. As you explore your curiosity about the Almighty, you begin to know God, and you also begin to get to know yourself more deeply. It is in this level of intimacy with the Almighty that eventually you begin to trust God. Take a moment to answer all your questions, to kill the thirst of your curiosity, and get to know God for yourself. When you do, you too will find that "indeed, the word of God is living and active, sharper than any two-edged sword, piercing until it divides soul from spirit, joints from marrow; it is able to judge the thoughts and intentions of the heart" (Heb. 4:12).

Reading the Bible is like reading any great novel. It really is a book full of stories about how others encountered God. The Bible allows us to get to know God's heart and how God works, so that God's word and our relationship with God become sharper than any other weapon we may use when we are going through. I have learned for myself that if I can "let go and let God," it is sharper than any rolling of my neck or trying to pay someone back for what she or he has done. It is sharper than my own way of doing things because, as we get to know God's heart, it ends up changing our heart as well. "Finally, beloved, whatever is true, whatever is honorable, whatever is just, whatever is pure, whatever is pleasing, whatever is commendable, if there is any excellence and if there is anything worthy of praise, think about these things" (Phil. 4:8).

If you don't believe it, check it out for yourself regarding those things in God's Word that make you go, "Hmm . . ." You might try reading the Bible in novel form. I highly recommend Walter Wangerin's *The Book of God.*

START THIS WEEK BY READING A STORY about one of the characters in the Bible. This book is based on Esther. Some other personalities in the Bible that you might explore are Noah, Ruth, Moses, and Abraham. Search your biblical character of choice via the Internet to see which one you would like to explore. Once you choose one, answer this question: How was God's hand at work in that person's story? Write your answer in the following space or in your journal.

WEEK 26

Solid As a Rock

A relationship that lasts, that is as solid as a rock, must be built on trust. What I mean by this is that your relationship must be based on an assured reliance on the character, ability, strength, and truth of the other person. And you don't just trust someone overnight; it takes evidence, patience, and time. You gather all the evidence you can and factor it all in to determine who this person is. You try to get to know the person's thoughts, words, and actions. You must put in the work to build the relationship so that over time you see the other's thoughts, words, and deeds and can take all of this evidence you have found to truly evaluate if this person deserves to be trusted. That's where the patience and time come in. So if you are going to trust, it definitely takes getting to know absolutely everything you can about the person. After you are assured as to who this person is and "ya like what ya see," you then move into what really becomes the glue that holds relationships together: trust. It is then that you can build the trust needed to make a relationship as solid as a rock.

If we are going to focus on faith, on a relationship with God, we must eventually ask, what is faith? Faith really is a belief in, or trust in, somebody or something. "Now faith is the assurance of things hoped for, the conviction of things not seen" (Heb. 11:1). But how do we believe in something or someone we cannot see? Well, I have heard an example that may help. When you go to the bank to deposit a check, you are taking a step of faith. You really have no guarantee that there are funds to back up that check, and yet you are presenting it to your bank on faith that you will get money from that check. As a matter of fact, there are tons of ways that we must believe in things we cannot see, and on what do we base our belief when we can't see? It is evidence. In this example you believe the person that gave you the check is good for the money, unless their behavior has said something different, right? If they have been bouncing checks from here to Mississippi, then you know that chances are you should not trust that the check can be cashed without bouncing. But if this person has given you the evidence, proof, verification, confirmation of character on which to base your belief that he or she is a trustworthy person, then you trust them, right?

How do you truly have a relationship if you can't trust the person? I know it would drive me *crazy* if I felt like I always had to check my husband's cell phone or pager to make sure he was not cheating on me. If you have no trust, your relationship is not built on a solid foundation. It is from this foundation that all other fundamental components of your relationship are built. So if you are going to focus on faith, you must first trust. "Trust in the Lord with all your heart, and do not rely on your own insight. In all your ways acknowledge him, and he will make straight your paths" (Prov. 3:5–6).

So after you feel like you know God for yourself and you have this relationship, the hardest thing to do is learning to let go and let God. What this really means is that in every decision, plan, or choice, seek God's counsel or advice—or, in some cases, realize that you just have to wait for a word as to what to do. Isn't that what you do when you are in relationship with someone? When you are doing something that will ultimately affect someone, isn't that person a part of the decision that you make? Well, our very lives affect God. After all, God did make us and, in seeking God, you are looking to ask, "Hmm . . . so what would *you* say that I should do about this?" Much like you would ask a parent or mate.

Perhaps you ask your mom's advice about this or that and you do that because you know your mom (or auntie or whomever you seek advice from) is not going to steer you in the wrong direction. Well, neither will God! Matter of fact, God will give you better advice than anyone else, including yourself, because God can see what is happening tomorrow while you are still in today.

It also means that you should—whatever you are dealing with or going through—acknowledge God. This means accepting that all these things that are happening are a part of God's plan for you and that all things work together for the good. Yes, even the bad stuff. So if you can just hang in there, you will eventually see God's plan for you. Here's an example. Have you seen the movie *Ray*, starring Jaime Foxx, about the life of Ray Charles? In the beginning of the movie, Ray, as a little boy, is just beginning to go blind, and he falls down and starts crying for his mother to help him (or something like that). His mother is right there in the room but she knows that the only way her blind son is going to make it in this world is for him to learn to get up for himself. So Ray's mom sits silently crying, watching her son struggle, watching him struggle newly blind, trying to navigate his surroundings. And little Ray does eventually get up on his own. Why does she do this? So that all things will work together for the good. So that Little Ray can learn how to find his way without anyone having to help him. His mother is looking at his future and not where he is right then.

Why is it so easy for us to worry or get anxious and not trust that even in the hard times God is at work for our good? Why is it so hard to just trust God? Are we saying that we really don't believe that God cares about us like a mother would for her child? For just as that mother did for her child, God has shown God's love for us and really does take care of every little thing in our lives. God really works best when we trust, if we can let go and let God, let God steer the ship instead of us trying to take the wheel. Now, if we are stubborn about something, God may let us try to take control, but then we want to blame God when it does not go right! Instead, as you build or renew your relationship, your challenge this week is to really begin to trust God, and out of the trust build a relationship that is solid as a rock. It is in this place that you can see how every event works together for your good.

Jesus said, "Everyone then who hears these words of mine and acts on them will be like a wise man who built his house on rock. The rain fell, the floods came, and the winds blew and beat on that house, but it did not fall, because it had been founded on rock" (Matt. 7:24–25).

IS IT HARD FOR YOU TO TRUST? If so, did something happen that has given you the inability to trust? Write it down.

WEEK 27

Is It Safe?

Think about it: fear is the absence of trust. When we feel fear, what is it we seek? To feel safe! Well, when there is trust in a relationship, you feel safe and secure in who the other person is, how this person will treat your heart, and his or her role in your life. When you feel safe, you can expose your most vulnerable self, knowing that this person will not take advantage of your opening yourself up. It is in this most vulnerable place that you can really let your guard down and begin to truly know a person's heart. It is in this most intimate place that the wall that most of us keep up to make us feel safe comes down, and you can allow this person to see you as your true self.

It's like taking your makeup off at night and allowing folks to see you at your most natural, your true self—you know, minus mascara, foundation, blush, and eyeliner. It is in this safe place that you can connect with others on a deeper level. So what does it really mean to feel safe?

Have you ever watched a child who is afraid of something? Like when you are at Disneyland and the big ole Mickey Mouse comes over, and a child is so terrified, he or she is running, trying to get away from Mickey. Yet if the parent picks the child up and takes him or her over to Mickey, that same child might just shake Mickey's hand.

What causes that child to feel safe in the parent's arms? It is because the child trusts the parent. But why does the child trust the parent? It is because the parent has shown that child that the parent will not let anything bad happen. So consider this perspective as we focus on faith: God has given us plenty of evidence on which to base our faith, our trust, in order for us to feel safe with God. It is the trust that comes from having a relationship with God. If we truly know God—God's character, God's love for us, God's Word—then we too can trust God to keep us safe from harm.

Let's look at it this way, again going back to a relationship to explain this concept further. If you are in a relationship and your partner tells you that he has lost his job, how do you respond? If he is able to be vulnerable with you, do you make him feel safe, or do you start that old rolling of the neck, going off because you can't pay your bills? Do you reassure him that you trust that he will find another job and that the two of you together will work everything out? This is what I call a safe place, where the two of you can be vulnerable regarding those big ole Mickey Mouses in the world, knowing you can find comfort and safety in each other's arms. It is this same comfort and safety that God provides for us.

Mary Stevenson has been credited with a well-known poem about a dream of walking along the shore with God. When times were tough, the two sets of footprints in the sand became only one set. The dreamer accuses God of abandonment during the tough times, but God replies that the one set of prints was actually when God was carrying the person.[16]

This is truly what I mean by a safe place—trusting that God has your back, that God will not leave you or forsake you. God will carry you when you can't carry yourself. You can anchor your life in the hope and promises that God brings to each of us. Our God is the well deep enough from which to draw peace, hope, wisdom, insight, love, endurance, and faith when you need it. When we need to be carried we must put our hope and trust in God . . . and let God do the rest.

SO THIS WEEK, ponder how you individually can find safety in the arms of God. You can write your musings here or in your journal.

Oh the comfort, the inexpressible comfort of feeling safe with a person, having neither to weigh thoughts nor measure words, but pouring them all right out, just as they are.

—Dinah Maria Mulock

Come to me, all you that are weary and are carrying heavy burdens, and I will give you rest.

—Matthew 11:28

WEEK 28

BLESSED ASSURANCE

When I think of all we have talked about in regards to building a relationship, trust, and feeling safe over the last few weeks, it makes me think of the old hymn "Blessed Assurance." For those of you who may not know it, it goes like this:

Blessed assurance, Jesus is mine!
O what a foretaste of glory divine!
Heir of salvation, purchase of God,
born of his Spirit, washed in his blood.

(Refrain)
This is my story, this is my song,
praising my Savior all the day long;
this is my story, this is my song,
praising my Savior all the day long.

Perfect submission, perfect delight,
visions of rapture now burst on my sight;
angels descending bring from above
echoes of mercy, whispers of love.

(Refrain)

Perfect submission, all is at rest;
I in my Savior am happy and blest,

watching and waiting, looking above,
filled with his goodness, lost in his love.

(Refrain)[17]

When I was little I would sing this in church with my grandmother, who sings *very* loudly and would totally embarrass me (just thinking of this makes me laugh out loud), so as a child I hated to hear this song. But now, as a grown woman, one who has fostered my own relationship with God, the words to this song have a whole new meaning. When I think of having trust and feeling safe in a relationship, it really means to have blessed assurance, to feel confidently assured that this person is who he says he is, will have your back, and has your best interest at heart.

When you are assured in anything, you are confident about that thing; you are not worrying if it will work out or if it is what it says it is or if people are who they say they are—you trust! Much like a basketball player does with members of the team, you are confident that your team members have skills and so you pass them the ball as you trust that they will do the right thing not just for themselves but for the team. When other players miss a shot, you don't lose your assurance, your confidence in their skills; you still know that they tried their best.

So if we apply this same blessed assurance to our relationship with God, we are safe and secure in who God is, for we know God is the same today, tomorrow, and forever. We know that God does not expect us to be perfect people but expects us to try our absolute best, and when we do, God will meet us where we are. Blessed assurance says that I am confident in who God is and what God has done, not just for me, but for others. It means that I have taken the time to get to know God for myself, having seen God move in my very own life. It is this movement that gives me my assurance, by way of confidence in who I am and the gifts God has given me. Let me put it this way, as Joyce Meyer said in her book *The Confident Woman:*

So, if I say I am confident, which I frequently do, I don't mean that I am confident in myself or my abilities. I mean that I am confident in my leader, God, and the gifts, talents, and knowledge He has placed in me. I know that without Him I am nothing (John 15:5), but with Him, I can be a champion, because He brings out the best in me.[18]

Just think about it: when you have confidence, you exude a certain aura. To have self-confidence is to feel like "I can do this!" instead of feeling like "I can't do anything." People will perceive that in you, and we all know that perception is reality. You can tell right off the bat if a woman has self-confidence or not. If you don't believe me, look at the comedian Monique; do you think she has self-confidence?

This talk of confidence and/or assurance is what some authors call the law of attraction. Your thoughts, emotions, beliefs, and actions attract matching positive or negative people, circumstances, and experiences in your life. Why do I bring all of this up now as we talk about our relationship with God? Well, confidence in self then dictates if we can be confident in the God who created us. You see, I believe that God created each of us uniquely, giving us each gifts, and it is up to us to relish the gift that we each are. As you delve into growing and learning about God, you can really begin to see who you are and become confident not just in yourself but in the God who has gifted you. So eventually we each come to our own time to shine.

So to walk in total "blessed assurance," we must believe in God as well as believe in ourselves. As my momma used to always say to me, "God don't make no junk!" which means we must believe that God created each of us special. God did not use a cookie cutter when making you, so find that special purpose God uniquely created inside of you. Some of us were called to be mothers, some teachers, preachers, doctors, lawyers, nurses, social workers, executives, and so on. I am a witness about this, for sure! When I began to grow in God, it was in that intimate place between God and me where I found my purpose! Little did I know that all things were really working together for my good. You see, God used everything I went through to get me to my time-to-shine moment, which became the first program of my nonprofit iDEFINE youth foundation, Imani Phi Christ.

[O]ur deepest fear is not that we are inadequate. Our deepest fear is that we are powerful beyond measure. It is our light, not our darkness, that most frightens us. We ask ourselves, Who am I to be brilliant, gorgeous, talented, fabulous? Actually, who are you *not* to be? You are a child of God. Your playing small doesn't serve the world. There is nothing enlightened about shrinking so that other people won't feel insecure around you. We are all meant to shine, as children do. We were born to make manifest the glory of God that is within us. It's not just in some of us; it's in everyone. And as we let our own light shine, we unconsciously give other people permission to do the same. As we're liberated from our own fear, our presence automatically liberates others.[19]

SO HERE IS YOUR THOUGHT TO PONDER THIS WEEK: What is your very own "blessed assurance"? What does your confidence rest on? What were you put on this earth to be or to do? What is *your* story, what is *your* song? Write your thoughts here or in your journal.

WEEK 29

PUT A RING ON IT

Once you get to a point in a relationship where you feel like you have really come to know the other person and you can feel safe and secure, when you have come to trust and love that person, your next natural step is to make a commitment or, as Beyoncé says, to "put a ring on it." When you "put a ring on it," or get engaged, you really are saying to your beloved, "After getting to know who you are and seriously exploring you, I want to share my life with you. Thus I am ready to make a commitment. This commitment means that I will cherish and protect our union, our partnership, and I am making a promise to strive toward building this relationship on a day-to-day basis. I am making a promise to share my life, love, dreams, desires, and world with you for the rest of my life."

Entering into a commitment like this with your mate usually starts first with an engagement ring, which says to the world and to you that you are working toward marriage. Once you "put a ring on it," you both enter a time of preparation toward your future together, which will include good times and bad, triumphs, challenges, and conflicts. "Research shows that there is a window of opportunity during the year before the wedding and the six months or so after when couples get the optimum benefit from marriage preparation. Later, under stress, negative habits and relationship patterns may become established and be much harder to resolve."[20]

Just as we enter this special phase in building a lifelong union with another person, so also we come to a similar phase in our relationship with God. We come to a point where we must make the decision that we want God to be a part of our lives and we are ready to walk with God 24/7. This step is an expression of the highest regard and a great compliment of love. Just as, when your partner offers you that ring he is saying that you have been placed as the highest priority in his life, the point you come to with the Almighty is no different. Treasure this commitment and use your relationship as a launching ground that marks the beginning of a new journey, which can take you to new places! New experiences! New heights! Just reading the following Bible verses makes me feel like I am entering again into this wonderful union with God:

> For surely I know the plans I have for you, says the Lord, plans for your welfare and not for harm, to give you a future with hope. Then when you call upon me and come and pray to me, I will hear you. When you search for me, you will find me; if you seek me with all your heart, I will let you find me, says the Lord, and I will restore your fortunes and gather you from all the nations and all the places where I have driven you, says the Lord, and I will bring you back to the place from which I sent you into exile. (Jer. 29:11–14)

Come to think of it, most of us believe that an engagement or wedding ring is a symbol of never-ending love, devotion, and commitment. So also "putting a ring on it" in regards to our relationship with God is a moment where you say, "Yes, God, I am ready to commit to having you be a part of my life as I walk with you daily, learning more about you and building a life with you."

However, before you take the big plunge into that marriage pool, there may be some things you need to work out so that you can fully commit to this relationship. So when that ring is coming and you are getting ready to say yes to the commitment, it is important to think about the commitment as much bigger than just a wedding; it is really starting a new life. Unfortunately, there are many who may say yes to the ring without even thinking beyond the wedding to actually prepare for a life together that will travel well beyond just that wedding day.

"Therefore shall a man leave his father and his mother, and shall cleave unto his wife: and they shall be one flesh" (Gen. 2:24 KJV). This is what I have heard many preachers call "leave to cleave." So if you are leaving your family to start you own family, it is critical that you take into account to whom you are going to cleave. The word "cleave," according to Webster's dictionary, means to adhere closely, stick, cling; or to remain faithful. Sometimes I wonder if we really take the time to think about what it means to cleave when picking our mate, for if we pick a mate based on looks or income, what happens when those things go? What happens when problems arise, when one of you loses a job, when you can't pay your bills, or when you need support to start your dream? What happens as your body ages, you get sick, or find out you have a life-threatening disease?

So just as we enter into our human marriage to build a lifetime and have one another's back through good and bad, this is the same principle we follow when we cleave to God. We may call it to "abide in God and God abide in us." This takes the relationship to a whole new level! By cleaving, sticking closely, we definitely begin to join into one flesh, one family, one purpose; this is indeed what it means to enter into a special place with God. You abide in this relationship by remaining stable, steadfast, and unyielding in your commitment.

> Abide in me as I abide in you. Just as the branch cannot bear fruit by itself unless it abides in the vine, neither can you unless you abide in me. I am the vine, you are the branches. Those who abide in me and I in them bear much fruit, because apart from me you can do

nothing. . . . My Father is glorified by this, that you bear much fruit and become my disciples. (John 15:4–5, 8)

It's almost like a man saying to his wife, "If you can trust me, I will do right by our family. Just have faith in the man you fell in love with and watch me give you everything you ever wanted." Shoot, if we can believe that from a man why can't we believe that from God? God has given us everything, and all God asks is that we "strive first for the [realm] of God and his righteousness, and all these things will be given to you as well" (Matt. 6:33).

AS WE DO, God will indeed give us everything. So as we enter this place where we "put a ring on it" and prepare to enter a union with the Almighty, the question to reflect on and write about this week is, how might you enhance your ability to seek God first in all that you do?

Unless commitment is made,
there are only promises and hopes; but no plans.
—Peter F. Drucker

WEEK 30

―

Can I Get a Rib?

"So the Lord God caused a deep sleep to fall upon the man, and he slept; then he took one of his ribs and closed up its place with flesh. And the rib that the Lord God had taken from the man he made into a woman" (Gen. 2:21–22).

As I was studying this Bible verse, the notes underneath this verse in my *Spirit Filled Life Bible* had this to say: "As in other creative miracles of scripture, God begins with a seed, such as the jar of meal from which Elijah ate for two and a half years and the fish and the loaves of bread with which Jesus fed the five thousand. The rib was likely chosen as representative of an intimate part of Adam's makeup."[21]

This makes me think of two things. It makes me think of seed time and harvest, and it also makes me think of becoming one with our mate as we get married. This idea of entering into relationship means joining with another. It is like bringing two pieces together to become a whole body, just as God did in taking Adam's rib to make Eve. So if we think of it this way, that God created each of us in God's own likeness or gave each of us a piece of *God's* rib, then we can look at this concept of becoming one with where our rib came from as a seed that has already been planted in us—a seed of faith, hope, love, and promise, a seed of the gift that becomes our purpose if we water it by exploring and learning about the *God in us!* Now that's the rib I am talking about!

"Do not be conformed to this world, but be transformed by the renewing of your minds, so that you may discern what is the will of God—what is good and acceptable and perfect" (Rom. 12:2). All God is really calling us to do is to keep our mind focused on that "rib" within. You see, if we can keep our mind focused on faith, hope, love, and promise, then we dwell in that special place where only God can dwell.

Okay, let me see if I can explain this further. The word "conformed" according to Webster's dictionary means to give the same shape, outline, or contour to; to bring into harmony or accord; to be similar or identical; to be in agreement or harmony. Isn't this what we strive for in any perfect relationship? So if we are having a relationship with God and are striving for what God strives for, we will heed Paul's words to the Philippians and think about "whatever is true, whatever is honorable, whatever is just, whatever is pure, whatever is pleasing, whatever is commendable, if there is any excellence and if there is anything worthy of praise" (Phil. 4:8).

On the other hand, when I think of what this Bible verse may mean by not conforming to this world, I think of all the things that have been developed that are not of God . . . the negative things of this world. Things like greed (if you don't know what I mean, think "Bernie Madoff"). Things like lust (if you don't know what I mean, think "Heidi Fleiss"). Things like jealousy (if you don't know what I mean, think "Tanya Harding"). If you surround yourself with greed, lust, jealously—then won't these negative things begin to infiltrate your being? However, if we transform and keep our minds renewed to the place where our "rib" came from, we then aspire to become more like God, which indeed is the opposite of the negative, the darkness of the world. It is living a life in the light. So this whole talk of the rib boils down to this: the way we live our lives will display what we conform to, who we are, what we are made of. It will show where your rib has come from—and that's what this whole personal relationship with God is all about.

Let me put it this way: when you mold a lump of clay, once it dries you *cannot* change the shape it has been molded into, right? In this same fashion our lives are being molded as well. As you conform or transform, that is, become what is around you (we will talk about your friends as we start part 5), if you choose to walk in the light and are transformed by renewing your mind, then so may you "discern what is the will of God—what is good and acceptable and perfect" (Rom. 12:2b) in your own life.

It is this most sacred place of your heart that is housed within your ribs. Yes, your ribs act as a fortress around your heart to keep it safe. And this too is the most intimate place that God can dwell. Thus if you are working to live a life focused on God instead of the world, then you will be headed in a positive direction as you transform yourself by this relationship you are having with the Almighty. It's kind of like those couples who have been married for a long time—you know how they begin to look alike and talk alike? Clearly this is what happens when we each spend time with God and form our own unique relationship. We begin to walk and talk differently, and this is what all of this rib talk is all about. When you are being your most positive, true self and are living in the light of your gifts, you truly are functioning just as God would have you function and that is why God created us . . . to be lights in a dark world!

> When we came to Christ in a moment of time our hearts became filled with light and our hardened, darkened hearts became softened, moldable, and usable pieces of clay in the hands of the Master craftsman. He then molds us and makes us into a beautiful, divinely changed piece of art. We then prove by the change in our lives to others what the good, acceptable, and perfect will of God is.[22]

So on the day that God used one of Adam's ribs to form Eve, it was a powerful statement of conformation and transformation, about becoming one with our maker. The thing we must realize is that although God gifted us with our rib, a seed of faith, hope, love, and promise, God has also given us the gift of free will. It is this gift that allows each of us to make our very own decisions, which we call choice.

SO ON THIS DAY, what will you choose? (Write thoughts here or in your journal.)

WEEK 31

—

LIFT THE VEIL

As we come to a close on the theme "Knowing God Intimately" and developing a relationship with God, we will conclude on the marriage topic we explored last week. In looking at the launching pad of marriage, the wedding itself, and walking down the aisle, what is the next thing that happens just after you say, "I do?" After you make that commitment to honor and cherish all the days of your life? The next thing that happens is you lift the veil. We all have heard the minister say to the groom right after the exchanging of the vows, "you may now kiss the bride," and then the groom lifts the bride's veil.

This tradition of a groom lifting his bride's veil after exchanging vows, as well as the following kiss, symbolize sealing the deal. This gesture symbolizes a connection, closeness—a bride and groom becoming one. Therefore this tradition of lifting the veil is a symbol of the relationship moving into a level of intimacy. And what is intimacy?

When I think of intimacy, I think of a familiar and very close connection with another as a result of having gotten to know and experience each other. True intimacy in relationships requires communication and vulnerability. It requires that you allow "in-to me-see" to get to intimacy. It is feeling comfortable enough to expose who you really are in a trusting, loving, secure place. It is closeness, tenderness, caring, and affection. It is sharing your most secret and private thoughts in a safe and comfortable place. It is mutual respect and recognition of each other's needs, wants, desires, hopes, and dreams. This place of intimacy is exactly the place where God dwells as we enter into a relationship with the Almighty. Let's take an even deeper look at this marriage to God.

"Wives, be subject to your husbands as you are to the Lord. For the husband is the head of the wife just as Christ is the head of the church, the body of which he is the Savior" (Eph. 5:22–23). Here is how my *Spirit Filled Life Bible* explains this verse:

As a wife, how should I behave toward my husband? Look to the chosen bride, the church, in its relationship with Christ; respect him, acknowledge his calling as "head" of the family, respond to his leadership, listen to him, praise him, be unified in purpose and will with him; be a true helper. Now, the Bible does not put males over females, but it does call for husbands to accept responsible leadership in the same spirit of self-giving and devotion Christ has shown for His church.[23]

Read for yourself all of Ephesians 5:22–33 and see quite a deeper meaning to Christ as the husband and the church as the bride. This scripture passage compares the relationship and responsibilities of the husband and wife to the relationship of Jesus and his church—which means *us*. In reading these verses you get to see Jesus' close and personal involvement in our lives, and you begin to realize that all God really wants is a passionate response from us to have such a relationship. He wants our undying devotion and commitment. Let's see if this will help our further exploration: "For I promised you in marriage to one husband, to present you as a chaste virgin to Christ" (2 Cor. 11:2b).

What is a chaste virgin? The word "chaste," according to Webster's dictionary, means pure in thought and act: modest. So if I were to define this chaste virgin I would say that God wants us to pursue this relationship with a pure heart. A heart that is not all mixed up with other things but is focused on God in all we do. It's just like when you work for a company and you always seek to do what is in direct alignment with the direction of the company's CEO, because you know if you do anything contrary, it may cost you your job!

Well, think of God as the CEO of your life. God has laid out a plan for each of our lives, a direction and focus, and if we can get under the covering of God's leadership, can you imagine the promotions we will receive?

This Bible verse makes it abundantly clear that the true church is the bride whom God chose to be wed to God's Son; therefore, if you are a Christian, then you are of the true church and, as such, you *are* "the bride of Christ." All Jesus desires is a relationship with his church of both intimacy and passion; of commitment and promise, just like a husband wants from a wife and any CEO wants from her or his employees. You know, the greatest passion and commitment to the company from employees creates the greatest long-term results for the company; therefore, these type of employees are always the ones who are being promoted.

Why? Because these are the folks who are passionately pursuing with diligence and determination the vision and purpose of the company. Why wouldn't God, the CEO of our company, our lives, want anything different out of us? God knows your gifts and desires because God put them in you. God also knows your hurt and pains, as well as your mistakes and your pitfalls. You can come to God just as you are. So lift the veil and allow Jesus, the bridegroom, to experience you and to mend your broken pieces.

Lift the veil and lay your passion and your desire, your hope and dreams at Jesus' feet. It is in this most intimate place that you build the most beautiful part of any relationship—that is what we call intimacy.

AS WE ENTER A NEW RELATIONSHIP or renew our relationship with God, it's time to walk down the aisle and lift that veil. As you do, in what ways can you begin to truly grow in your intimacy with God? Jot your thoughts down here or in your journal.

*What makes humanity so desirable
is the marvelous thing it does to us; it creates
in us a capacity for the closest possible
intimacy with God.*

—MONICA BALDWIN

PART FIVE

Iron Sharpens Iron

WEEK 32

—

Iron Sharpens Iron

Throughout the last several weeks we concentrated on our relationship with God; now our theme becomes our relationships with those around us. The question you must first ask yourself is whether your friends and/or family are making a positive contribution to your life. Or are they planting weeds that will ultimately steal your thunder and kill your dreams? *We really only want people around us who will support our dreams and push us into being our greatest self.* These are the folks who are going to tell us what we need to hear, instead of what we want to hear, people who will keep us on our toes while at the same time being on their toes themselves. These friends have to be just as sharp as you are aiming to be. "As iron sharpens iron, so one [wo]man sharpens another" (Prov. 27:17 NIV). Now in our modern age, we could say that steel sharpens steel.

The point is that you become what you surround yourself with. You know that popular saying "birds of a feather flock together"? People really do grow from their interactions, dealings, and relationships with others. The group of folks around you can help you to grow in a positive direction or do the exact opposite. The key for you to win at this game of life is to have the right group of folks playing on your team, to sharpen you as you equally sharpen them.

Have you ever actually seen how iron or steel gets sharpened? A knife, for example, is not sharpened by a napkin, a towel, a piece of bread or a plastic or wooden cutting board. A knife may cut these things or cut on these surfaces, but over time the knife dulls and it must be sharpened. You all know how you put that knife in the back of the can opener and it starts to sharpen it. Well, if you look back there, don't you see the same material that the knife is made out of sharpening it? You see that a type of metal is used to keep a knife sharpened so that it is bright, sharp, and ready to do what it needs to do (and the sharper it is, the better). Just as the sharper we are the better, right? So why would we not want to have people around us who keep us sharp?

What happens when we have folks around us who do not sharpen us? It's like those big Hollywood stars that have all the "yes" men around them. You know, the stars that go broke or become addicted. Even when I think of what happened to Michael Jackson, it makes me think that if the brotha would have had some friends around him keeping him sharp, they would have been saying, "No, Michael, you cannot stay on this drug!" "No, Michael, you can't keep taking that, it's going to kill you!" Instead he had folks around him that were not sharpening him; instead they were giving him whatever he wanted. This is not the kind of folks you want or need around you. If Michael Jackson had had a different set of folks around him, he might still be alive today. "Whoever walks with the wise becomes wise, but the companion of fools suffers harm" (Prov. 13:20).

Now, in no way am I saying that Michael Jackson's death is the fault of those around him, but I am saying that if you have the right group of people around you, it will help you make better decisions, wiser choices. They will give you informed alternatives and intelligent insight as well as constructive criticism and intuitive analysis on every action or decision you make in your life. Who does not want that? We must be very strategic about the folks we allow to play on our team. After all, why do you think the NBA or NFL is so picky about whom they draft? Because they only want players who will play to win. They only want players who will have informed alternatives and give intelligent insight to the plays that need to happen for the team to win. Don't you want the same thing for your life?

"Two are better than one, because they have a good reward for their toil. For if they fall, one will lift up the other; but woe to one who is alone and falls and does not have another to help" (Eccl. 4:9–10).

So having the right friends, the right team, is a *wonderful* thing! Friends ought to sharpen and improve each other. They share success and are there to pick one another up when either of them falls. They have complementary personalities, talents, and skills so that were one is weak, the other may be strong. It does not mean that you always get along, but, at the end of the day, you know that a true friend always has your back and is there to defend you against the opposing team—the haters!

The question here is: who are the people closest to you? Your sista girls, mentors, confidants, and even your mate—are they helping you to grow? Are they giving your wise counsel and support? It's time to take a look at the folks around you to make sure you have a Shaq and a Kobe on your team to help you play to win!

TAKE A MOMENT TO REALLY THINK about your closest group of friends. Are they helping you to win at the game of life or are they taking you off your focus? Who might you need to let go so that you can be better and do better? You may want to jot some names here or in your journal.

Keep away from those who try to belittle
your ambitions. Small people always do that, but the really
great make you believe that you can become great.

—MARK TWAIN

Don't walk in front of me; I may not follow.
Don't walk behind me; I may not lead. Just walk
beside me and be my friend.

—ALBERT CAMUS

A friend is someone who knows the song
in your heart and can sing it back to you when
you have forgotten the words.

—UNKNOWN

Much of the vitality in a friendship lies
in the honoring of differences,
not simply in the enjoyment of similarities.

—UNKNOWN

True friendship isn't about
being there when it's convenient;
it's about being there when it's not.

—UNKNOWN

WEEK 33

Do unto Others

You know, when I think of the kind of people I want to have around me, it makes me think of the golden rule: "Do to others as you would have them do to you" (Luke 6:31).

With this in mind, I would like to share with you the ingredients of what I call my friendship soufflé. These are the factors that I believe, if mixed just right, make for a great friendship, a great team to help you move toward your dreams:

MY FRIENDSHIP SOUFFLÉ

One Cup of Being Real

I cannot stand folks who are fake, so honesty is huge for me. After all, how do you know if someone is truly your friend if that person is always changing so that he or she will be liked or accepted by other people. Instead, be who you are! I would not call this person a friend but rather an opportunist. At the end of the day, this person is not being authentic or honest to herself, let alone you as a friend.

Two Cups of Being Loyal

If my friend tells me something in confidence, I keep that information to myself. After all, nobody likes a backstabber. In this same vein, I don't talk behind my friends' backs. If you are a true friend you never say anything about your friends that you could not say to them face to face. On top of all of that, you also must not allow others to say bad things about your friend either. A true friend has your back and speaks up for you when the haters are doing what they do best—hating!

Half of a Tablespoon of Don't Wear Out Your Welcome

When I was little my mother used to always say, "Don't wear out your welcome" when I went to a friend's house, and now I get it. This is all about knowing your boundaries and making folks feel appreciated. Boundaries are important! For example, did your girlfriend give you permission to reprimand her child? Just because you think her kids should be raised a certain way does not give you the right to step over that boundary. So be mindful that this is her life, don't offer unsolicited advice, and don't say or do things to her kids or her man that are not within her own bounds. Also, don't help yourself to things at her house without asking, unless she can do the same at your house. If you borrow something from a friend, return it before that friend has to ask you for it, and make sure you take good care of it. What else? Don't make your friends feel like they are being used! Give and take equally.

A Liter of Keep Your Promises

Do what you say you are going to do! My pet peeve is when someone doesn't. If you know you said you would be there at 7 and it is 7:15, call and explain why you are late. Don't just keep a sista hanging! If you made a promise and then circumstances happen beyond your control, let your friend know. It's better to call and tell her what is going on than to leave her in the dark, thinking that the original plan is still on. Good friendship is based on trust—if you break a friend's trust, that part of your friendship may be very hard to rebuild.

Two Tablespoons of Being There

If you sense that your friend is having a particularly hard week, offer to help. Go by and watch the kids while she goes to get a pedicure. If she is sick, take her some soup. Send cards and care packages. The point is, care enough about your friend to be there through it all, the good and the bad! Sometimes when a friend is going through, there are no words to say, but knowing you are there is all a friend needs.

Five Cups of Agree to Disagree

In a friendship you *must* understand that you will not always see eye to eye, and it is in these moments that you must realize it is okay to disagree. I don't have to get all mad at you because you are not seeing things my way! Friendship really is accepting each other's differences as well as appreciating what you have in common. It is the differences of each of your friends that make them each uniquely who they are. Sometimes those differences can make things uncomfortable! However, if you can agree to disagree, one minute you can be in a heated discussion, the next minute you are both letting it all go and on your way to grab lunch. Now that is the pinnacle of friendship!

THE POINT OF THIS FRIENDSHIP SOUFFLÉ is that you always want to treat a friend as you would want to be treated. To do this you must be the same kind of friend you are seeking in a friendship. What are some of the ingredients in your friendship soufflé? Write down those ingredients you expect to receive while at the same time equally giving as a great friend.

*The great difference between voyages rests
not in ships but in the people you meet on them.*

—AMELIA BURR

*To have a good friend is one of the highest delights
of life; to be a good friend is one of the noblest
and most difficult undertakings.*

—ANONYMOUS

The only way to have a friend is to be one.

—RALPH WALDO EMERSON

WEEK 34

To Whom Can You Turn?

This whole talk about looking at the people around you boils down to one thing: to whom can you turn? Who is there when you need them the most? You see, if we each are heading to our very own "for such a time as this" moment, just as Esther did, we need to know that we have people in our corner whom we can call on in our time of need. Esther had people around her who fasted and prayed with her as she came to one of the most important decisions in her life.

So this whole talk of iron sharpening iron is not just about being like-minded, but also about those friends who are with us when all is not going well. You know, when you lost your job, you call the friend you can tell who won't say, "Hmm, what did you do this time?" When your man is acting up, it's that friend to whom you know you can go cry on her shoulder, and who makes you feel like you can make it through this. You all know what I am talking about, those friends that will go with you through the fire!

SO WHAT FRIENDS OR FAMILY do you know who will absolutely be there for you when you need them? List their names here or in your journal.

Lots of people want to ride with you in the limo,
but what you want is someone who will take the bus
with you when the limo breaks down.

—OPRAH

REAL FRIENDS

A simple friend has never seen you cry.
A real friend has shoulders soggy from your tears.
A simple friend doesn't know your parents' first names.
A real friend has your phone numbers in her address book.
A simple friend brings a bottle of wine to your party.
A real friend comes early to help you cook and stays late to help you clean.
A simple friend hates it when you call after he has gone to bed.
A real friend asks you why you took so long to call.
A simple friend seeks to talk with you about your problems.
A real friend seeks to help you with your problems.
A simple friend wonders about your romantic history.
A real friend could blackmail you with it.
A simple friend, when visiting, acts like a guest.
A real friend opens your refrigerator and helps herself.

A simple friend thinks the friendship is over when you have an argument.
A real friend knows that it's not a friendship until after you've had a fight.
A simple friend expects you to always be there for him/her.
A real friend expects to always be there for you!
A simple friend will read and throw this letter away.
A real friend will send it back to you until s/he's sure it's been received.

—AUTHOR UNKNOWN

It's the friends you can call up at 4 A.M. that matter.

—MARLENE DIETRICH

The firmest friendships have been formed
in mutual adversity, as iron is most strongly united
by the fiercest flame.

—CHARLES CALEB COLTON

Adversity not only draws people together
but brings forth that beautiful inward friendship.

—SØREN KIERKEGAARD

WEEK 35

The Outer Realm

Over the last few weeks we have looked at all of the folks who make up your team. There are two other types of friendships I want to discuss. This week we start to look at the first of the two, the outer realm. Many times a relationship—whether with someone who started out as your best friend in high school, or your childhood friend from the neighborhood, or just someone who has been your confidant—can change over time.

The outer realm is made up of those friends who may not necessarily have a positive affect on your life, but their intention is definitely not to have a negative one. Yes, we all have issues, but those people in your outer realm are the ones whose issues can negatively affect you if you let them get too close, whether or not this is their intention. This is the sista who always has drama going on in her life and whose lack of self-esteem keeps her stuck in a nonmoving situation. It's like there is a dark cloud hanging over her head, hanging over her life, and this cloud has the ability to suck the life right out of you as well if you allow it. Now don't get me wrong, the friends that you move from your inner circle to the outer realm may not be bad people, and maybe this particular "outer realm" friend is just going through a rough patch. But when that rough patch moves from affecting just her to hurting you, all because her negative vibe is transferring onto you, this means you have got to make room enough not to let her negativity infiltrate your positive spirit.

I am in no way saying to close the door to those friends who may not be quite up to par to be in that "inner circle" of your team. Maybe they are just not capable of being on your team at this moment. Perhaps this person's issues are just temporarily overtaking her life and she just may not be at the capacity yet to be on your team because of this. One day she may get it together and then be ready to become a member of your team. *The difference between these folks and the haters is that this group is trying to do better, they just aren't there yet.* So be the kind of friend to her that you would want as well. You can be the light at the end of the tunnel, telling your friends in the outer realm or in the audience at your game of life to stop being so negative. Hold them to their greatest potential while at the same time keeping enough space between the two of you so that their negative "woe is me" does not pull you down too. You know, nurse the friend with a cold without catching it from her.

So how do you know when to move a friend from the inner circle to the outer realm? This can be tricky, as there is also a third category—those who are drinking the hater-ade. These are the ones we must learn to let go—we will begin to discuss this in a few weeks. But for now, really think about the direction in which your life is headed. Who are the people who will help you move in this direction, and who are the folks who will keep you stuck in a nonmoving position? Now think of those who keep you from moving but don't do it on purpose. They don't mean to do this, they just can't see beyond where they currently are to see the possibility in their own lives, let alone in yours. This is the group we are talking about. It may indeed be your light that may be just what a friend in this group needs to move her from the drama into possibility.

PONDER THIS WEEK how you might help those in your outer realm to see the light while not becoming hindered yourself and sucked into their darkness. If you like, jot down your thoughts here or in your journal.

*There is nothing more dreadful than the
habit of doubt. Doubt separates people. It is a poison
that disintegrates friendships and breaks up pleasant
relations. It is a thorn that irritates and hurts;
it is a sword that kills.*

—LORD BUDDHA

Never let the hand you hold, hold you down.

—AUTHOR UNKNOWN

*A true friend never gets in your way unless
you happen to be going down.*

—ARNOLD GLASOW

*The most beautiful discovery true friends make
is that they can grow separately without growing apart.*

—ELISABETH FOLEY

WEEK 36

———

THE POWER OF THE WIND

"You can't control the winds, but you *can* control how you set your sails" (Yiddish proverb).

This quote really got me thinking about the wind and the power of something that we cannot see but definitely can feel. Wind can be as large as a tornado, destroying homes and wiping out cities, or as small as someone blowing at a piece of paper on a table. After a little exploration, I found that the wind was mentioned in the Bible quite a few times. Here is a notable verse: "And suddenly from heaven there came a sound like the rush of a violent wind, and it filled the entire house where they were sitting" (Acts 2:2).

This really got my curiosity going, so I looked up what wind means. Webster's dictionary says it is a force or agency that carries along or influences, but it also says that wind is a destructive force or influence. After reading these two definitions I realized that, in terms of our direction in life, it comes down to this: we must really look at the type of wind our friends blow into our life. We really need to assess for ourselves if their wind is moving us in a positive direction or is a destructive influence in our lives.

Webster's dictionary also said wind is "spirit" or "breath." Thinking about that Bible verse I just quoted made me wonder more about the Holy Spirit, and so I began to explore that topic and found: "Do you not know that you are God's temple and that God's Spirit dwells in you?" (1 Cor. 3:16).

So it is this wind, this spirit of God that dwells in each of us. The question we must ponder is, might the wind of those around us increase this wind that dwells in us or decrease it? Think of it like this: God allows for each of us to have our own free will. It is this same free will that gives us what we call choice—the choice to water the seed of the Spirit that dwells within so that it can grow and prosper or the choice to allow destructive winds to come in and take over that dwelling. You see, the problem with wind is that you can't see it, and so you must *really* be mindful of what is happening around you. You have to know at all times to what direction your sail is set so that if wind comes in that is contrary to sending your boat in that direction, you can reset your sail so you continue to move in the direction of your purpose, your dream, your goals. For if you get sucked into a destructive gale or tornado, you will not be able to see clearly enough to find your way out, and thus you *will* lose your direction. So stand back and look at what is happening around you and what is happening around your friends. Get to know in which direction their wind blows!

"For what human being knows what is truly human except the human spirit that is within? So also no one comprehends what is truly God's except the Spirit of God" (1 Cor. 2:11).

It boils down to discerning what kind of spirit lives inside your friends. It is that wind, that spirit, that then translates into where they are headed and all that is produced in their lives. "Thus you will know them by their fruits" (Matt. 7:20).

THIS WEEK PONDER THE DIRECTION your friends are headed and the fruit that is produced by them. Just as you can identify a tree by its fruit, so you can identify people by their actions. You can identify them by the winds that blow in their life, so sit back and take a look at their actions to assess in what direction their wind blows. You can jot some notes here or in your journal.

If a man does not know what port he is steering for,
no wind is favorable to him.
—SENECA

The pessimist complains about the wind;
the optimist expects it to change;
the realist adjusts the sails.
—WILLIAM ARTHUR WARD

The answer, my friend, is blowin' in the wind.
The answer is blowin' in the wind.
—BOB DYLAN

WEEK 37

Understanding There Will Be "Hateration"

Unfortunately, no matter how hard we work on improving ourselves and staying positive, there will always be someone who is hating on you for who you are and where you are headed. You know, those people who just can't stand to see you doing well. I know from experience that it is very hurtful when someone starts to flip the script on you. If you don't know what I mean, let me ask you this: have you ever felt like one of your friends or family members might be jealous of you? But you dismiss the thought because you think to yourself, "how could I think such a thing?" Well, guess what, maybe you weren't wrong when you thought so! Some of the very people who you think are in your corner really aren't. Believe it or not, some folks do *not* want to see you happy. Or at least they are fine just as long as you are not happier or doing better than they are.

Why does this happen? To understand why some people become a hater over time we must look at what it is to be jealous. Jealousy really begins with *how a person feels about herself or himself.* Dare I say, it comes from a person's own insecurity or lack of self-confidence? Jealousy people aren't at all happy with themselves.

So in essence jealous people are so dissatisfied with themselves that they try and make you feel or look lower than they are so that they can feel better. Now, let's face it, we all get a little jealous sometimes. However, when that jealousy turns into something that is hurtful, humiliating, back-stabbing, and/or demeaning, then it is has turned into what I call "hateration."

At the end of the day, jealously comes from a want for something you don't have or a feeling like you can't measure up and, over time, becomes a struggle for power. So think about this: you may indeed be giving power to the person who is jealous of you by feeding into this dissatisfaction of self. We do this when we find out that a friend is talking about us behind our back, so we in turn start to talk about them. This becomes a tit for tat that gives negativity control over your life. For it takes much more energy to be negative than it does to be positive. When people act out of feelings of jealousy, they are in essence trying to exert power over something they feel they are threatened by or something that has been taken away from them. So if you try to get back at them, you are just feeding into this power struggle. You are feeding into the negativity. Do you remember the movie *Gremlins*? If you feed a gremlin, it is just going to grow bigger and bigger.

Could it just be that your friend has become jealous because you are climbing in the direction of your dreams and she is not? Why is it that some women cannot just congratulate each other when they are doing well instead of getting jealous? We all must realize that we really can learn from one another and grow if we can stay positive and remember that *your* gift is not *my* gift! A *true* friend should support you. Sometimes you can help a jealous friend conquer her insecurities, but other times it's best to cut all ties and let her go. What we must do when we come to the crossroad of insecurity, envy, covetousness, and hateration is to really figure out for yourself whether your friend would be more secure if she had what she envies or if she'd just find something else to be jealous of. It really is a thin line between someone who is having a temporary woe-is-me moment or having a case of what I like to call the negativity tornado. If it is the negativity tornado that just keeps blowing and blowing and blowing in a whirlwind, you *must* let this person go.

"Beware of false prophets, who come to you in sheep's clothing but inwardly are ravenous wolves. You will know them by their fruits. Are grapes gathered from thorns, or figs from thistles? In the same way, every good tree bears good fruit, but the bad tree bears bad fruit. A good tree cannot bear bad fruit, nor can a bad tree bear good fruit. Every tree that does not bear good fruit is cut down and thrown into the fire. Thus you will know them by their fruits." (Matt. 7:15–20)

YOUR MISSION THIS WEEK is to *really* figure out what friends are lifting you and what friend are tearing you down. Take a moment and understand who has caught the hateration bug!

When people show you who they are, believe them.
—OPRAH WINFREY

WEEK 38

Learning to Let Go

If you have people in your life who are mad at you because you are doing better, jealous because you are excelling, or hating because you have a new life goal, stop making your life miserable and let them go! Did you know that relationship conflict and stress have been shown to have a negative impact on your health, raising your blood pressure and contributing to heart disease? That's why it's in your best interest to decrease or eliminate negative relationships in your life. Ladies, it is time to stop allowing the crabs to try and pull you back into the barrel; *let them go!*

"Do not be deceived: Evil company corrupts good character" (1 Cor. 15:33 NKJV). Keeping negative, harmful, depressing, and destructive people in your life will produce negative, harmful, depressing, and destructive results. If you want positive, constructive, affirming, encouraging things to occur in your life, you should surround yourself with these types of people, places, and things. Remember, negative produces negative, and positive produces positive.

First, know that you must initiate the letting go. Sometimes we stay in friendships way past their expiration dates—and you know what happens to things past their expiration date? They spoil! They smell bad and if we try and eat or drink them, they make us sick. So wouldn't this apply to a relationship that has run past its course? Just like that sour milk, we've got to pour it down the drain . . . we have got to let it go!

So how to do it? The key to letting go of any bad relationship is first to get the issues out in the open. If you address the situation, you'll save yourself a great deal of drama and stress that you would have if you kept it all inside. By putting the issue on the table for a nice healthy discussion, you will either clear up any confusion or you will see who this person really is.

Start the conversation by being open and honest about your feelings, but avoid laying blame or charging the other person with things, avoid being mean or rolling your neck—just focus on you and how you feel in a nice and positive spirit. If you approach this conversation negatively, then it will definitely be negative. But if you come with positive intentions, and it turns negative anyway, you will know that it is not you. Give your friend an opportunity to share his or her feelings, listen to what he or she has to say, but also pay attention to the things the person doesn't say.

Now after you have this conversation, gradually separate yourself. Speak less on the phone, see each other less, and begin to withdraw slowly. This will give you the space to see things clearly, and it will allow your friend to ruminate on your conversation. After all, if you keep doing things the same way you used to, then she or he may not take your conversation seriously. What do you do next? Sit back and see what happens. Your friend's behavior will speak volumes. Remember that quote from Oprah, "When people show you who they are, believe them."

Second—once you have taken the initiative and had the "letting go" conversation with the other person—you must allow God to work. I am sure you have heard the saying, "Let go, and let God." This letting go is an act of surrender, surrender to the fact that we actually have no control. We cannot control how people act and the decisions that they make. Instead of fighting "what is," we need to learn to accept and to be at peace. All we *can* control is how we allow others' actions to affect us and how we interact or react to them. By choosing to have peace, and trusting that what is meant to be shall be, we can hold on to more of a positive outlook about whatever comes our way. By letting go, we actually allow more positive energy to flow to us instead of trying to force what may not be meant to be—if it doesn't fit, don't force it.

Whatever happens, know that all things in life, including friendships, change over time. Some folks grow with you; some folks grow in other directions. The act of letting go is really standing up for yourself as you exercise your right to be respected not just by others but by and for yourself as well. By letting go, you are taking back the control of your life as you DEFINE how you will and will not be treated. By letting go of bad company, you free yourself to be the *you* that you deserve to be!

AS HARD AS THIS EXERCISE WILL BE, write down the names of who you truly need to let go of that you are holding on to, thinking and hoping that they will be better and do better.

We all lose friends. We lose them in death, to distance,
and over time. But even though they may be lost, hope is not.
The key is to keep them in your heart, and when the
time is right, you can pick up the friendship
right where you left off. Even the lost find their
way home when you leave the light on.
—Amy Marie Walz

WEEK 39

—

WHAT KIND OF FRIEND ARE YOU?

So as we close out on our discussion about iron sharpening iron, the last question, which summarizes what we have discussed, is what kind of friend are you? The focus must also be on how you treat your team. So as you begin to let go of the negative folks, it is also important that you make those who lifted you up feel valued and appreciated. You must not only know how to utilize them to uplift your life and not take advantage of them, but you also must know what they need from you. We must invest in our relationships. Making people feel appreciated is the key to maintaining friendships.

So what kind of friend are you? Think about it. Do you let your friends know how much you treasure, cherish, and respect their roles in your life? If your team is supporting your goals, you have to support their goals equally. Remember a relationship is a two-way street and therefore not all about you!

"Do to others as you would have them do to you" (Luke 6:31). Just as you expect from your friend, you be the same kind of friend. On the same token, we have to understand who our friends are. Some friends are phone people; some are not (like me). You see, I am the worst with calling folks back, and all my friends know that. I will meet you for a meal or e-mail you all day long, but my memory is the worst, and my schedule during any given day may not always allow me to call folks back. If you know that about me, you know you are better off e-mailing me if you want to track me down. Get to know who your friends are! Some need a call when they are going through a rough patch; some do not. The only way you know these things is to really understand that each of your team members are all individual people who all make unique contributions to your life. Knowing their role or their position (like in basketball) on your team will only benefit both of you in a relationship. Then you will not expect a friend to do things she is not capable of doing, and vice versa. The key to a lasting friendship is accepting who each other is . . . that is what I call love.

> Love is patient; love is kind; love is not envious or boastful or arrogant or rude. It does not insist on its own way; it is not irritable or resentful; it does not rejoice in wrongdoing, but rejoices in the truth. It bears all things, believes all things, hopes all things, endures all things. (1 Cor. 13:4–7)

So while many people think of love as just a feeling, it is also a choice. It is something you must decide to do and to give every day. It is given out in the ways we act and react to all those we interface with, and it is especially tested when you come to areas of disagreement. You see, when we accept people for who they are, there will also be areas that we may not come in alignment with. This area of disagreement is usually where your conflicts, your misunderstandings will fall. Ultimately in times of discord, the art of acceptance and not taking things personally comes into play. In a friendship you should be able to agree to disagree and move on from a heated disagreement. You should be able to let it go and still go to the mall and enjoy your afternoon, even though you disagree about something.

"Love one another with mutual affection; outdo one another in showing honor" (Rom. 12:10). In other words, honor who your friends are who may have different opinions and outlooks on things but love you just the same! Sisterly or brotherly love is a gift we give to others. It isn't purchased by actions or contingent on our emotions. It is based on mutual respect, caring, and sharing. It is based on support and encouragement. It is based on giving and receiving. It is based on honoring who each other is and the role we play in each other's life.

TODAY, THINK ABOUT WHAT KIND OF FRIEND you are. In what ways can you improve your role in a friendship? Are you too demanding or do you understand exactly who each of your friends is and expect each to be no one else but who she or he is? Jot down your responses.

No person is your friend who demands your silence,
or denies your right to grow.
—ALICE WALKER

The most beautiful discovery true friends make is that they
can grow separately without growing apart.
—ELISABETH FOLEY

True friendship is seen through the heart,
not through the eyes.
—UNKNOWN

Be courteous to all, but intimate with few, and let those few
be well tried before you give them your confidence. True friendship
is a plant of slow growth, and must undergo and withstand the
shocks of adversity before it is entitled to the appellation.
—GEORGE WASHINGTON

PART SIX

Give to Others

WEEK 40

It Takes a Village

The saying "It takes a village to raise a child" is an African proverb. Upon further investigation I found out that it originated from the Nigerian Igbo culture and proverb "Ora na azu nwa." Thinking about this proverb reminds me of growing up in my community of South Central Los Angeles in the 1970s. When I was growing up, anyone from my neighborhood at any given time could reprimand me if I was bad or would invite me into their home for milk and cookies.

My neighbors were my babysitters when my parents needed to go somewhere. My mother would make a call and off I ran up the street to play with my friends while my mother went to the store. Or I would spend a day or two if my parents were traveling out of town. We often went over to our neighbors to celebrate birthdays or other milestones in our community. So the phrase "it takes a village" takes me to the memories reminding me it was not just my mother and father raising me but my whole "village" who made contributions. It is sad to realize that this same community/village is rarely seen in today's society. As a result, what is happening to our children?

It's not that parents are working longer hours or are far less attentive to their children, but that our village concept has disbanded. It was this village that helped pick up the pieces when parents needed that extra hand. It is sad to say that, in the world today, entrusting anyone other than well-known family or friends help with the rearing of our children could lead to hazardous results. If you don't believe me, think of Elizabeth Smart or the countless children who have been abducted, kidnapped, or snatched. It is sad but true, the bad things that can happen to children these days, and it makes me wonder, what happened to our village?

I believe this African adage, "it takes a village," is the work I continue through Imani Phi Christ as we become the village that works hand in hand with parents to raise their children. I started this program because I know how important my village was to my growth and development. "Two are better than one, because they have a good reward for their toil" (Eccl. 4:9).

But it seems that this helping one another, this reaching out to teach and bring up children in the entire community has shifted over time, and with it has also shifted the landscape of our community. It shifted from marching together, fighting together, and believing that no man is an island to people living on their own islands, even when they live right next door to you.

Hillary Clinton, when she was serving as First Lady of the United States, used the phrase "It takes a village" for the title of the book she wrote presenting her vision for the children of America. She focused on the impact that individuals and groups outside the family have on a child's well-being, and she advocated for a society that would meet all of a child's needs. So if a child can become a more responsible citizen by having caring and supportive adults in his or her life, why aren't more becoming the village our young people today need?

It is interesting how in today's world we are so focused on impressing others with our possessions or abilities that we often do not stop long enough to give to others so we can also make a difference in the world around us. This is what I think of when I hear "It takes a village." We will explore over the next weeks how we can become much more community focused.

THIS WEEK THE QUESTION TO PONDER is, in what ways are you helping your village?

A healthy social life is found only
when in the mirror of each soul the whole community
finds its reflection . . .
—RUDOLF STINER

Men exist for the sake of one another.
Teach them then or bear with them.
—MARCUS AURELIUS ANTONINUS

The challenge of social justice is to evoke
a sense of community that we need to make our nation
a better place, just as we make it a safer place.
—MARIAN WRIGHT EDELMAN

WEEK 41

—

S I T - I N S ,   M A R C H E S ,   A N D   M O V E M E N T S

When I think of the African adage "It takes a village," it takes me back to memories of all the sit-ins, marches, and movements of the 1960s. It makes me think of how so many of different races and ethnicities banded together to bring attention to unequal treatment. Had we not banded together at that time, imagine where black folks would be today. If we had done nothing to fight for equal rights, it would have meant that we were accepting the status quo of the way we lived as well as all the injustice and inequity that existed here in the United States.

Coming together as a village during the sit-ins, marches, and movements not only made a stronger force in the fight for our rights, but it also served to form a positive image of the black community. Our village came together as a people to find ways to put an end to the segregation that was apparent in this country. The sit-ins and marches of the civil rights movement helped blacks to regain strength as a people, and they caused the country to uphold the equality and justice of all people.

If we take this concept into modern times, how might sit-ins, marches, and movements impact our village today? Sure, we may have more access to opportunity, but so many of our youth are dealing with a whole different set of shackles than those who came before them. In the 1960s the fight was about access to jobs, homes, income, education, voting. Although today's issues are different, sometimes I think we have forgotten about the struggle or that we think the struggle is over. But I dare to say that the struggle continues. It continues for those who can't find employment and fight poverty every day. It continues for the young woman who finds herself living in a hopeless existence and can't seem to find her way out. It continues for the woman with three kids she is struggling to raise alone, with no mate and no village to help her. It continues for the youth who join gangs, sell drugs, and do this because they know no other way. I can go on, but we must come together to fight for today's call for freedom, freedom from our current oppressor—whatever the dilemma is that keeps so many from living to their full potential. It saddens me to think of our youth who are falling by the wayside in dramatic proportions. Many of them have no vision for the future, are dropping out of school, and are suffering from teenage pregnancy, gang violence, drug sales, and/or abuse. Think about how powerful it would be if we all banded together to overcome these modern-day shackles. After all, our youth *are* our future, and what legacy will be left if we do not help them now?

For me, growing up in South Central Los Angeles was not a roadblock because I had a village around me that held me accountable and called me out when I was wrong. However, today this village is barely speaking out when our kids don't have textbooks in our schools, let alone anything else. Now I don't mean to get on a soapbox, but I see this all over the country as I travel to work with our chapters of Imani Phi Christ. Our young people need us like never before. Unemployment numbers are skyrocketing. Human trafficking is at an all-time high, and not overseas but here in America! Our community is crying out for us to hear, and to act.

And so the first question that the priest asked, the first question that the Levite asked was, "If I stop to help this man, what will happen to me? But then the Good Samaritan came by, and he reversed the question: "If I do not stop to help this man, what will happen to him?"[24]

Think about it: if Esther never stopped to stand in the gap for her people, what would have happened to them? In what ways can we each carry the torch of our ancestors, those who came before us, and all that they went through, so that others can?

THIS WEEK THE QUESTION TO PONDER is this, how can you be of service to those in need all around you? How can you extend your hand to the village that needs you now?

Imagine what a harmonious world it could be
if every single person, both young and old, shared a little
of what he is good at doing.
—QUINCY JONES

When you help someone up a hill,
you find yourself closer to the top.
—BROWNIE WISE

Each one, reach one. Each one, teach one.
Until all are taught.
—MARK VICTOR HANSEN

WEEK 42

—

LOVE YOUR NEIGHBOR AS YOURSELF

All of this talk about our village and how we can truly give to others makes me think of one of the first Bible verses I ever learned, "You shall love your neighbor as yourself" (Matt. 19:19b NKJV).

This is actually one of the Ten Commandments, and when I explore this commandment there are two words that stick out for me, "love" and "neighbor." We are to treat our neighbor the way we treat ourselves—but just who is our neighbor?

When you think of the word "neighbor," the first thing that comes to my mind is the person who lives next door or maybe on the same block, but for some reason I don't think that was all this verse meant by "neighbor." Hmm . . . what did Jesus mean here? Here's another verse that I think will answer that question:

> "You have heard that it was said, 'You shall love your neighbor and hate your enemy.' But I say to you, love your enemies and pray for those who persecute you, so that you may be children of your Father in heaven; for he makes his sun rise on the evil and on the good, and sends rain on the righteous and the unrighteous. For if you love those who love you, what reward do you have? Do not even the tax collectors do the same? And if you greet only your brothers and sisters, what more are you doing than others? Do not even the Gentiles do the same? Be perfect, therefore, as your heavenly Father is perfect." (Matt. 5:43–48)

So what we are really called to do is love *everyone* as our neighbor. What I gather from this Bible verse is that we should not differentiate how we care for others based on social status, economic background, race, and so on. Instead, if we love others as ourselves, then we should treat them exactly as we would like to be treated! This is the Golden Rule: "Therefore, whatever you want men to do to you, do also to them . . ." (Matt. 7:12 NKJV).

The Golden Rule puts this whole "love your neighbor as yourself" concept into action. It boils down to serving others. We all remember someone telling us at some point in our lives to help others in need, not because we have to or because we are seeking some reward but because we see a need. In doing so, we are looking beyond situation and circumstance through the eyes of unconditional love, the same unconditional love that God has for each of us. Now, this is not to say that we could ever fully emulate God, but we are often told that God is our example to follow.

Have you ever heard of that popular saying, WWJD (What would Jesus do?)? So what would he do? When I think of who Jesus is, I think of meeting people where they are. I think of compassion, understanding, love, sympathy, caring, benevolence, and concern. The most valuable lesson I take from this look at loving your neighbor as yourself is that it is calling each of us to be just as Jesus would be—kind, considerate, and compassionate to others. It is not sitting in judgment or rejecting folks because they are different. It is not our place to make assumptions or to criticize others; after all, that would contradict what it means to have compassion and understanding, and it is this compassion and understanding that ultimately is what loving your neighbor as yourself is all about.

HERE'S OUR QUESTION FOR THE WEEK TO PONDER: in what ways can you become a better neighbor? How can you enhance your inner compassion and understanding? Not just to the folks who live next door or on your block, but how can you extend the African adage "It takes a village" and become part of a village that uplifts, upholds, sustains, supports, encourages, and empowers all? What are ways you can live in service to others?

Teach us, good Lord, to serve you as you deserve:
to give, and not to count the cost,
to fight, and not to heed the wounds,
to toil, and not to seek for rest,
to labor, and not to ask for any reward,
save that of knowing that we do your will."

—IGNATIUS OF LOYOLA

WEEK 43

Who's Gonna Check Me Boo

This has to be one of my favorite sayings from the TV show *Real Housewives of Atlanta*. Now, while I have grown to not like how women are portrayed on these shows, I just love to say this line! I really do try to find any reason to say it, because it makes just about anyone I say it to laugh. But in thinking about it, if I was seriously using this line it really would mean that I am saying, "It's all about me! It's all about me!" Hmmmm . . . isn't this saying symbolic of the "I, me, mine culture" we currently live in? We, at all costs, "look out for number one." You know, we say things like "Have it your way," "I gotta look out for me," and now we can add to that "Who's gonna check me boo."

So many of us think we are all too important. We are too busy to let a car in when we are driving down the street, too much in a rush to speak to the girl at the counter in the supermarket, don't have enough time to stop and speak to the receptionist at the school when we are picking up our kids. Many have complained about folks (especially our youth) and their growing lack of respect for one another, let alone the world around them. Some say it is all due to the hip-hop culture and those daggone music videos. Others say it's everyone's stress level because of the economy. I say it's just straight-out selfishness. These days, folks are just plain old comfortable with being selfish! We will help someone only if it somehow benefits us. We are polite only if we have to be or if we know this person is "somebody" and being polite to them now will somehow help us later. Now, while there is nothing wrong with making sure your needs are met, we cannot stop there. We must also think beyond ourselves to the needs of others. You never know when a simple hello can brighten someone's day. To live a life all and only about me would mean that I live a very selfish existence as if no one else mattered and I really do not care. It would mean that I am concerned only with myself, seeking or concentrating on *my* advantage, *my* pleasure, or *my* well-being without regard for others. How can we live in a world that solely focuses on self?

"For the Son of Man came not to be served but to serve, and to give his life a ransom for many" (Mark 10:45). When I think of what Jesus did for all of us, I think of him as certainly not focusing on self. I think of what he did as an act of love. And, when you think about it, love and selfishness are complete opposites, as love is focused on others and selfishness is focused on self. Hmm . . . and pride and selfishness go hand in hand. They are both focused all on I, me, and mine. To take it a step further, pride and selfishness produce strife and disharmony. Could this indeed be what has happened to our village over time? Selfishness and pride have taken over!

"By insolence the heedless make strife, but wisdom is with those who take advice" (Prov. 13:10). It's time for us to move from the strife of pride and this "I, me and mine" mentality to live a life in service and love toward others. So when I say, "Who's gonna check me boo," it is really a call for us all to check ourselves, our neighborhoods, our friends, and our families. It's a call for each of us to rally around the needs of others. To take some soup to a sick friend, feed the homeless, plant a tree, visit the sick and shut in, be part of a community clean-up, mentor a young person, send a donation to a charity—the list is endless, the ways you can give your time, talent, and/or treasure to help enhance the life of others.

So this week's "Who's gonna check me boo" is a call for an attitude adjustment, to stop just thinking about that new outfit for that party this weekend, or how you can network yourself into that new position, or even that cute guy you met yesterday—but to really look at how we can increase the landscape of our world. It is time to turn our focus from fancy cars and shiny gems to clean neighborhoods, health care for all, access to quality education for every child. It's time to turn our efforts to stopping the violence in our communities and making it known that no man or woman should hit or hurt one another! It is time for us to see beyond just self to see how we can each lift up and enhance the environment we live in.

Now don't get me wrong, there is nothing wrong with wanting nice things. But we must not just think about ourselves any more. Check yourselves, ladies. Wake up and let's all see what the needs are around us. It's time to give back!

IN WHAT WAYS MIGHT YOU NEED to check yourself and realize the needs that are occurring around you, open your eyes and see how you can serve and give back so that others too may be lifted up? How can you live in service to others?

You will rise by lifting others.
—Robert Green Ingersoll

Service to others is the rent you pay for your room here on earth.
—Muhammad Ali

*Every day I live I am more convinced that the
waste of life lies in the love we have not given,
the powers we have not used, the selfish prudence
that will risk nothing and which, shirking pain,
misses happiness as well.*

—MARY CHOLMONDELEY

*Wisdom ceases to be wisdom when it
becomes too proud to weep, too grave to laugh,
and too selfish to see others than itself.*

—KAHLIL GIBRAN

WEEK 44

GOTTA GET YOUR SERVE ON

When I first think of the word "serve," it makes me think of being subservient, docile, being made to be ignorant, having to bow down, and being less than. However, on the other end of this serve continuum is this:

> Whoever wishes to become great among you must be your servant, and whoever wishes to be first among you must be your slave, just as the Son of Man came not to be served but to serve, and to give his life a ransom for many. (Matt. 20:26–28)

In other words, those who seek power and position would do better to approach leadership as a servant. Jesus himself was a gift to the world as he came to serve and to give to us and not to receive from us. Jesus even becoming flesh was an unselfish act for us all. So what does it really mean to serve? We will look at it through what I call the three ingredients of servitude, which are (1) a giving spirit, (2) humility, and (3) a pure heart.

When I think of someone who has a *giving spirit*, I think of someone who gives of him- or herself to benefit others. It is the mother who gives up her career to stay home with her kids; however, it is also the mother who works 9 to 5, comes home to cook dinner and bathe her kids, reads them a story at night, and tucks them in, even though she is worn out from the day's stress. It is about finding your talent and passing it on. It is making time when you don't have it and giving it anyway. It is lending a hand even when you are tired and worn out. It is thinking beyond yourself to meet another's need that may be greater than yours. It is an act of love that is a gift that keeps on giving.

Humility of mind knows that everything is not about you. Instead you look for ways to be of service to others. "My speech and my proclamation were not with plausible words of wisdom, but with a demonstration of the Spirit and of power, so that your faith might rest not on human wisdom but on the power of God" (1 Cor. 2:4–5).

It is the God in you that shines forth in the act of seeking beyond self to the needs of others. So, in essence, you do not focus on all your accolades and honors, your jobs or your titles, but you let your light shine as you give of your talents in service to others so that they too may be lifted up. For even Jesus humbled himself and became flesh, and, to take it a step further, you did not hear of Jesus walking around saying, "Do you know who I am?" Instead you found him with the prostitutes and tax collectors. He humbled himself and met people where they were. Because he served those who were forgotten, they were able to see the God in him.

A pure heart moves our focus toward the inner person—the heart. A pure heart serves without motive. There is no hidden agenda. There is no focus on doing the right thing even for the right reasons, but instead an authentic desire to serve, to help others. "It is more blessed to give than to receive" (Acts 20:35).

Let me see if I can summarize all three of these concepts. To be a servant is the highest honor. Yes, everyone wants to be in some kind of important role, to be a leader. Nobody wants to be a follower. But leadership, the position and power, should not be our focus. Robert K. Greenleaf coined the term "servant leader" in "The Servant as Leader," an essay that he first published in 1970, where he had this to say:

The servant-leader *is* servant first. . . . It begins with the natural feeling that one wants to serve, to serve *first*. Then conscious choice brings one to aspire to lead. That person is sharply different from one who is *leader* first, perhaps because of the need to assuage an unusual power drive or to acquire material possessions . . . . the difference manifests itself in the care taken by the servant, first to make sure that other people's highest priority needs are being served.

In his second major essay, "The Institution as Servant," Greenleaf said:

Caring for persons, the more able and the less able serving each other, is the rock upon which a good society is built. Whereas, until recently, caring was largely person to person, now most of it is mediated through institutions—often large, complex, powerful, impersonal; not always competent; sometimes corrupt. If a better society is to be built, one that is more just and more loving, one that provides greater creative opportunity for its people, then the most open course is to raise both the capacity to serve and the very performance as servant. . . .[25]

Doesn't Greenleaf just say it all! A better world *can* be created by each of us making our highest priority serving the needs of others. Servant leadership is, indeed, what makes our world a better place for *everyone*, and the reason why it is important for us to each improve our serving. That is, we each must find for ourselves a giving spirit, humility, and a pure heart—the ingredients to cultivate our servitude—as a gift we each give to the world.

THE QUESTION FOR THIS WEEK IS, how do you need to shift the priorities in your life to make this a major concern? Write down the ways you can accomplish this.

> *No person was ever honored for what he received.*
> *He was honored for what he gave.*
> —CALVIN COOLIDGE

> *Everybody can be great.*
> *Because anybody can serve.*
> *You only need a heart full of grace.*
> *A soul generated by love.*
> —MARTIN LUTHER KING JR.

> *I've learned that people will forget what you said,*
> *people will forget what you did, but people will*
> *never forget how you made them feel.*
> —MAYA ANGELOU

WEEK 45

—

REACHING BACK TO PULL UP

How did you make it to where you currently are? Was it a college scholarship you received? An introduction someone made? A sacrifice a parent gave? Whatever it was, each of us is where we are because of a resource we received or because someone helped us get there. When I look back over my life, I think of all the things people have done for me that have helped me to make it to the place where I currently stand.

I remember my YMCA summer camp counselor, Cheryl, whom I met when I was twelve years old, and what having her as a mentor meant to me. I remember my boss, the producer at BET (Black Entertainment Television), Sheila, who said to me one day, "What do you want to do? You work too hard for this job," and she made a phone call that was an introduction for me that changed my career path. I remember my pastor, Rev. Dr. Cecil L. "Chip" Murray, who took me under his wing when I was a young twenty-something-year-old starting a program. He believed in me and encouraged me in ways that helped me to grow. Yes, of course, family members have helped me too. I remember how my mother *made* me go to church every Sunday. But I also remember how that small nudge instilled in me the importance of faith. I remember my Aunt Faye and how I admired her independence, which sparked in me the notion of being an independent woman. I remember my dad and my uncles, who made me feel like such a lady and showed me how a woman should be treated by a man.

I could go on, but the point is, each of these people as well as countless other friends, bosses, neighbors, mentors, and family became my village as they poured into my life. It was because they each gave to me that I am the woman I am today. So as we close our section on focus number 5, "Giving Back," it is time for us not only to reflect on the various people and/or resources that have helped us, but also to pay it forward.

That's what it means to reach back to pull up. It is remembering those who reached back to us and pulled us up and continuing to give to them by giving to others along the way. You know, for me it really is because someone reached back and pulled me up that I find myself doing the same for others today. I strive to reach back and give back through the work I do with Imani, as well as by being a mentor, a friend, a wife, and a stepmother. Reaching back and pulling others up also means carrying the torch of our ancestors as we each continue to march along on life's highway, partaking in the hope and opportunity so many before us fought for, so that we could have what we have today. My village carried the torch as they helped me stay on my path, just as yours did for you. I pray that I too am effectively helping others, as others are still helping me.

Some of you may be saying that no one has ever given anything to you. So does that mean you don't give anything to anyone else? Consider what Jesus said: "Do to others as you would have them do to you" (Luke 6:31). "Give, and it will be given to you. A good measure, pressed down, shaken together, running over, will be put into your lap; for the measure you give will be the measure you get back" (Luke 6:38).

The bottom line in this discussion is that we *all* should give, and be happy to do so. Are you a cheerful giver? Do you look for opportunities to give, share, help, encourage others? It is in the act gift of giving that we reap the benefits. Giving not only feels good to the heart, it enriches the soul as God pours out blessings back to us for the gift(s) we give to others.

SO AS WE LEAVE THIS TOPIC, look back over your life and think about how you made it. Think of ways to continue to carry the torch so that others too can come up behind us—that indeed is reaching back to pull up.

Do not neglect to do good and to share what you have,
for such sacrifices are pleasing to God.
—HEBREWS 13:16

How does God's love abide in anyone who
has the world's goods and sees a brother or sister
in need and yet refuses help? Little children, let us love,
not in word or speech, but in truth and action.
—1 JOHN 3:17–18

The point is this: the one who sows sparingly
will also reap sparingly, and the one who sows bountifully
will also reap bountifully. Each of you must give as you have
made up your mind, not reluctantly or under compulsion,
for God loves a cheerful giver.
—2 CORINTHIANS 9:6–7

PART 7

Let Your Light Shine

WEEK 46

———

LET THERE BE LIGHT

When you think about light, what do you think of? Sun on your face? A flashlight showing you the way? A switch flipped on in a room so that you can see? But let's think bigger and further back than these examples. Light was the beginning of everything! "Then God said, 'Let there be light'" (Gen. 1:3a).

This is the first command God gives in the Bible. The verse just before this one, Genesis 1:2, says that "the earth was a formless void; and darkness covered the face of the deep." *So everything began with light.* Even we began with light. A light of purpose and promise was planted inside of each of us at birth. This seed of light then goes through life's circumstances and situations and, if we navigate successfully through them, we learn the lessons that only life teaches us, so that our light may begin to shine.

It's almost like our light is what a silversmith is looking to see when he or she is processing silver. They hold that piece of silver over the fire and let it heat up, because in order to refine the silver, one must hold the silver in the middle of the fire where the flames are hottest to burn away all the impurities. Could it be that life's situations and circumstances happen to each of us to burn away impurities so that we can shine that much brighter?

So, ladies, it is indeed this same light that each of us emits when we are fully present to the self that God made us to be, despite the situations and circumstances that try to hinder us from being we are meant to be! Yes, this would mean that you overcome, and you know who you are, and therefore your switch is flipped on, and you *shine* for the world to see. "For it is the God who said, 'Let light shine out of darkness,' who has shone in our hearts to give the light of the knowledge of the glory of God in the face of Jesus Christ" (2 Cor. 4:6).

So what is this light in us? I believe it is being our most positive self and walking in the light of our gift that God has given to each of us. This is what you do when you know who you are and what you are good at, and you live and perform in that greatness that is uniquely yours and yours alone. This is how you begin to grow and expand, and, as you do, you also grow in your relationship with God.

"Again Jesus spoke to them, saying, 'I am the light of the world. Whoever follows me will never walk in darkness but will have the light of life'" (John 8:12). You see, it is the Creator who made each of us with our own special purpose. As we expand in God, God can expand in us. That, indeed, is the source of the light! This is how we flip on the switch! Over the course of this book, together in our discussions, we have carved out a course toward living in your own light! "But if we walk in the light as he himself is in the light, we have fellowship with one another" (1 John 1:7a).

My prayer is that, along the course of this year, your light has begun to shine that much brighter because you have defined your way that much more distinctly.

SO TAKE SOME TIME TO EXPLORE: what is your light? If you don't know, e-mail or call three of your closest friends and ask them this: If they had to define you in one word, what would that be? Write the answers they give you here or in your journal.

You are the light of the world.
A city built on a hill cannot be hid.

—MATTHEW 5:14

So that you may be blameless and harmless,
children of God without blemish in the midst of a
crooked and perverse generation, in which you
shine like stars in the world.

—PHILIPPIANS 2:15

We are told to let our light shine and if it does,
we won't need to tell anybody it does.
Lighthouses don't fire cannons to call their attention
to their shining—they just shine.

—DWIGHT MOODY

I am not bound to win, but I am bound to be true.
I am not bound to succeed, but I am bound to live by the light
that I have. I must stand with anybody that stands right
and stand with him while he is right and part
with him where he goes wrong.

—ABRAHAM LINCOLN

We cannot hold a torch to light another's path
without brightening our own.

—BEN SWEETLAND

Faith is the strength by which a shattered world
shall emerge into the light.

—HELEN KELLER

Flip on Your Switch

"In the same way, let your light shine before others, so that they may see your good works and give glory to your Father in heaven" (Matt. 5:16).

I believe that when we are born God gives each of us a gift, and this is what I call your greatness! My gift is not the same as yours. Now, to be fully present in your gift and therefore living in your light, you must be able to answer one question, *why are you here?* Have you found your passion, do you live in your purpose and love what you do? When you do, then your light is on, and it is time for all of us to flip on our switches to truly live into all that we are meant to be and do.

I would even venture to ask you, have you found fulfillment in your career? My desire is that everyone finds the happiness I have found when I stumbled on and found my purpose. To find this for yourself, you have to understand what I call the GPS of defining your purpose:

> G—GROW your GREATNESS (to do this you must realize your GIFTS and talents).
>
> P—Discover your PASSION PROFESSION.
>
> S—Create a plan to SHINE in your career and in life.

I am sure you can guess from earlier in our journey that I love to use a GPS when I need direction. And defining your purpose is really about knowing where you want to end up, truly knowing what your gifts and talents are, and creating a life using your gift. It is really using your own personal GPS to move you in the direction of your life's purpose.

Yes, it is that simple! So if you aren't in the land of passion and purpose, I am calling you to a defining moment like the one I had many years ago when I flipped on my switch to live in my own light. It's time for you to start the journey to live the life that you were born to pursue. It's time for you to define your purpose! It's time for you to flip on your switch and live in your own light!

THIS WEEK, STOP AND THINK about whether you are truly doing and being *all* that God created you to be.

WEEK 48

EXPAND YOUR TERRITORY

All this talk of letting your light shine makes me ask the question, "Are you really pushing yourself to grow deeper and deeper in your greatness? Are you expanding your territory?" After all, what would be the point if you wanted to be a better you and all of this work was not going to make you stronger, larger, and increase and develop a deeper you?

"Jabez called on the God of Israel, saying, 'Oh that you would bless me and enlarge my border, and that your hand might be with me, and that you would keep me from hurt and harm!' And God granted what he asked" (1 Chron. 4:10).

There is a small book called *The Prayer of Jabez* by Bruce Wilkinson about what happens when ordinary folks decide to reach for the extraordinary in life. Basically this book asks, "Do you want a bigger vision for your life?"[26] Wilkinson was asked the same question by his seminary teacher, only after that question he asked another question, "Will you sign up to be a gimper for God?" If you are like me, you are probably saying to yourself, what the heck is a gimper? As his professor explained it to him, a gimper is someone who always does a little more than what's required or expected. Just as Jabez did. "Jabez was honored more than his brothers" (1 Chron. 4:9a).

So to truly expand your territory, you must do a little more than what is expected, right? That is exactly what the prayer of Jabez is talking about. When we are born, we are each given gifts.

Some of us know what they are and are working in them; some of us are not. Some of us know what they are, but we allow fear, hurt, resentment, or thinking that we aren't ready or don't have enough time or money to start working within our gift right now to keep us from using our gift. Well, if we all thought that way there would be no Oprah, no Barack Obama, there would be no Tyler Perry, no Cornell West. There would be no Beyoncé, no Raven Simon; there would be no doctors, lawyers, counselors, or teachers. There would be only plain do-only-your-job kind of folks instead of folks like Marva Collins, who started her own school in her home so that black children could receive a quality education. My point is that whatever your gift is, whatever you are good at, whatever you are called to do, it is time to expand your territory and do it well! Go over and above just being mediocre and do it phenomenally! Yes, a phenomenal woman is what each of us should be!

> If it falls your lot to be a street sweeper, sweep streets like Michelangelo painted pictures, sweep streets like Beethoven composed music, sweep streets like Leontyne Price sings before the Metropolitan Opera. Sweep streets like Shakespeare wrote poetry. Sweep streets so well that all the hosts of heaven and earth will have to pause and say: Here lived a great street sweeper who swept his job well.[27]

You see, just as Jabez wants to succeed and increase his sphere of influence for God, you can increase your sphere of influence for God by becoming all that you were meant to be. How? Well, when you are being the most positive person you can be, when you are letting nothing or no one hold you back and are truly exercising your gifts, do you know what happens? You shine! "In the same way, let your light shine before others, so that they may see your good works and give glory to your Father in heaven" (Matt. 5:16).

It is important for us to take note that the prayer of Jabez was also Jabez calling himself to a higher self and a closer relationship with God. It is time for each of us to make a commitment to not just work toward but to *be* all we were created to be. To give God glory in *all* we do. To let our lights shine for the whole world to see.

THE QUESTION FOR THIS WEEK IS, in what ways shall you expand your territory? In what ways will you take your shine to the next level?

Shoot for the moon. Even if you miss,
you'll land among the stars.
—Les Brown

Success isn't a result of spontaneous combustion.
You must set yourself on fire.
—Arnold H. Glasow

Life's problems wouldn't be called "hurdles"
if there wasn't a way to get over them.
—Author unknown

God gives us dreams a size too big
so that we can grow into them.
—Carine Roitfield

You have to expect things of yourself
before you can do them.
—Michael Jordan

WEEK 49

THIS LITTLE LIGHT OF MINE, I'M GONNA LET IT SHINE!

With Queen Esther as our example, together we have taken a journey toward finding our very own time-to-shine moment. The greatest lesson that we learn from Esther is what happens when preparation meets opportunity and what happens when we move past our fear and allow faith to be our guide. Indeed, all things are possible! My prayer is that, over the course of this year, you have found your own light as you defined, designed, or re-designed your course; stepped out of your own darkness; let go of the past and/or the negative people, circumstances, and situations; and are now shining as you light the path for yourself as well as for others to come behind you. So it is definitely time for us to live in our own light! All we have to do is reach for it—reach to be the best you can be, and then flip it on! Flip on that switch. It is already there. Let your light shine so brightly that folks have to put on their sunglasses to be around you! Be all that God made you to be! This is exactly how we each get to our very own "for such a time as this" moment.

So it's time to stand in the light of who you are and what you are good at, the light of the roles you play as friend, daughter, sister, wife/girlfriend, mother, business owner, college student, or whatever. If you are not fully present in your light, what might you do in order to let your light shine? In what ways are you brighter and better and in what ways can you consciously push yourself to let your light shine even more?

"You are the light of the world. A city built on a hill cannot be hidden. No one after lighting a lamp puts it under the bushel basket, but on the lampstand, and it gives light to all in the house. In the same way, let your light shine before others, so that they may see your good works and give glory to your Father in heaven" (Matt. 5:14–16).

I want to leave you this week with this quote by Marianne Williamson, which you read in week 28 but which bears repeating:

[O]ur deepest fear is not that we are inadequate. Our deepest fear is that we are powerful beyond measure. It is our light, not our darkness, that most frightens us. We ask ourselves, Who am I to be brilliant, gorgeous, talented, fabulous? Actually, who are you *not* to be? You are a child of God. Your playing small doesn't serve the world. There is nothing enlightened about shrinking so that other people won't feel insecure around you. We are all meant to shine, as children do. We were born to make manifest the glory of God that is within us. It's not just in some of us; it's in everyone. And as we let our own light shine, we unconsciously give other people permission to do the same. As we're liberated from our own fear, our presence automatically liberates others.[28]

It is time to be able to say (repeat after me) *This little light of mine, I'm gonna let it shine!* So go on and let it shine, let it shine, let it shine!

IN WHAT WAYS DO YOU BELIEVE you are allowing your light to shine bigger, better, brighter? What are ways that you can continue to turn your switch up so that over time you can be as bright as you can be?

PART EIGHT

Lock in the Learning: Exploring Your Journey

WEEK 50

What Did You Learn?

These last two weeks are an opportunity for you to lock in what you have learned. Go back through the book and be reminded of all that you have learned during our journey together.

Go back and review your journey by reading your notes and your answers to the questions. As you do, stop and answer these additional questions:

- What have you learned about yourself over the journey of this book?
- What goals did you set for yourself?
- How have you grown and expanded?
- What have you let go of to stay on your course? What will you do to keep negative things off of you as you journey through life?
- Who are the members of your team who will help you play to win at the game of life?
- What is your new plan to have time for intimacy with God?

EACH YEAR IS AN OPPORTUNITY for you to water the seeds of your greatness and become a better YOU! What did you learn about your greatness as you read this book?

WEEK 51

Setting Intentions

Now that you have gone back and put together all that you have learned over the course of reading this book, what do you intend to do with what you have learned?

This week's exercise is much like what you did with your vision board, where you set intentions for yourself. I encourage you to review your notes from week 8. Sit with all that you have learned and set SMART goals for yourself—goals that are specific, measurable, attainable, realistic, and time-focused.

NOW THAT YOU KNOW MORE ABOUT YOURSELF and are determined to grow, what do you intend to start today to grow your greatness?

WEEK 52

I'm Coming Out!

I really wish you could see me doing my happy dance! My happy dance is about you moving in the direction of expanding, growing, molding, and exalting your *greatness*! A song that Diana Ross recorded in the 1980s (yes, I am dating myself) is the absolute perfect way to commemorate our time together. She sings, "I'm coming out, I want the world to know . . . I got to let it show."[29]

Think of this chapter as a celebration of your coming-out party! Coming out to be *all* that you were meant to be—like a caterpillar emerging to become a beautiful butterfly! I pray that by now, as you became deliberate and intentional about growing your greatness, you have emerged as a more vigorous, amazing, empowered, brilliant, fabulous, phenomenal, dazzling *you*! It's time for you to live in your purpose lane and move toward your dreams, goals, and desires! I hope you have discovered that life brings lessons to make you better, stronger, and wiser, just as they did for Esther. The lessons aren't over. And remember, *all* things (not just some) work together for good as you work toward your time-to-shine moment!

Please do not hesitate to allow me to serve you in further growing your greatness. My life's calling is to encourage and empower you to find and define the absolute greatest life for you. To see what ways I may continue this journey with you, I invite you to see my website at www.NicoleRobertsJones.com.

WOO-HOOO! I am so excited for you! Do and be all that you are meant to be as you show the world your shine!

NOTES

Note: Quotations at chapter ends, unless otherwise noted, are taken from ThinkExist.com, Quotations (1999–2006), http://thinkexist.com.

INTRODUCTION

1. I explored the Book of Esther in depth in 2005 for my own personal Bible study time. I found the following resources invaluable in guiding my journey, particularly Charles Swindoll's book: Charles R. Swindoll, *Esther a Woman of Strength & Dignity* (Nashville: Word Publishing, 1997); Dianne Sagan, "Women of the Bible—Esther," Protestantism @ Suite 101 (2007), http://dianne-sagan.suite101.com /women-of-the-bible-esther-a28116#ixzz1tzkcxGWB; and Got Questions Ministries (2002–2012), "Book of Esther," http://www.gotquestions.org/Book-of-Esther.html. I relied considerably on these sources while writing about Esther in this book.

WEEK 2: YOU WILL WAIT

2. Marian Wright Edelman, *Lanterns: A Memoir of Mentors* (Boston: Beacon Press, 1999), 118.

WEEK 3: LET'S CALL HER STRENGTH AND DIGNITY

3. From Luke Easter and Dee Cheeks "A Strong Woman vs. a Woman of Strength," http://www.poemsabout.com/poet/luke-easter/. Used by permission of Luke Easter.

WEEK 5: I WON'T TAKE NOTHIN' FOR MY JOURNEY NOW

4. "Keep Your Eyes on the Prize," lyrics attributed to Alice Wine (1956). Tune "Gospel Plow" (also known as "Hold On"), traditional American folk song (Roud Folk Song Index, number 10075). Recorded by Pete Seeger, Bruce Springsteen, and others, http://www.acousticmusicarchive .com/lyrics-chords/traditional/american/205-eyes-on-the-prize.

WEEK 6: WRITE THE VISION

5. Stuart Warner, "The Reticular Activating System," make-your-goals-happen.com, http://www.make-your-goals-happen.com/reticular-activating-system.html.

WEEK 7: IT'S LIKE A BOOMERANG
6. Ruth Krauss, *The Carrot Seed* (New York: Harper Collins, 1973).
WEEK 10: BEGIN WITH THE END IN MIND
7. Stephen Covey, *The 7 Habits of Highly Effective People* (New York: Free Press, 1989), 99.
WEEK 14: DON'T LOOK BACK
8. Sidney Poitier, *Measure of a Man: A Spiritual Autobiography* (San Francisco: HarperCollins, 2000), 292.
9. Joel Osteen, *Become a Better You* (New York: Free Press, 2007), 173.
WEEK 15: DID YA LEARN SOMETHING?
10. Rick Warren, quoted in "Learning lessons from life's hurts," by Jennifer Riley, *Christian Today,* posted March 30, 2009, www.christian today.com/article/learning.lessons.from.lifes.hurts/22941.htm.
WEEK 17: WHO HAS YOUR REMOTE?
11. Elizabeth Scott, "Develop An Internal Locus of Control," About.com, February 22, 2012, http://stress.about.com/od/psychological conditions/ht/locus.htm.
WEEK 18: I FORGIVE YOU
12. Fred Luskin, *Forgive for Good: A Proven Prescription for Health and Happiness* (New York: HarperOne, 2003), vii–viii.
13. Tim Laurence, quoted in Jane Collingwood, "Using Forgiveness to Move On," *PsychCentral,* 2012, http://psychcentral.com/lib/2007/using-forgiveness-to-move-on/.
14. Marie Speed, "Maya Angelou: Voice of Our Time," *Success* magazine, www.success.com/articles/1515-maya-angelou-voice-of-our-time, accessed 10/11/2012.
WEEK 21: BE AN EAGLE
15. Author unknown, "Soar Like an Eagle," found on numerous blogs and devotional websites, including http://www.doodlespage.com/soar.html.
16. Mary Stevenson, "Footprints," 1984, from original 1936. The poem may be read online at http://www.footprints-inthe-sand.com/index.php?page=Poem/Poem.php.
WEEK 28: BLESSED ASSURANCE
17. Fanny J. Crosby, "Blessed Assurance," 1873, lyrics and music at http://library.timelesstruths.org/music/Blessed_Assurance/.
18. Joyce Meyer, *The Confident Woman* (Nashville: FaithWords, 2006), 7.
19. Marianne Williamson, *A Return to Love: Reflections on the Principles of a Course in Miracles* (New York: HarperCollins, 1992), 164–5.

WEEK 29: PUT A RING ON IT

20. Patty and Greg Kuhlman, "Is Premarital Counseling or Education for You?" WedAlert.com, 2011, http://www.wedalert.com/content/articles/premarital_counseling.asp.

WEEK 30: CAN I GET A RIB?

21. Jack W. Hayford, ed., *Spirit Filled Life Bible* (Nashville: Thomas Nelson, 1991), 8.

22. Adam Chinnock, Sealed in Jesus (2000–2002), www.sealedinjesus.com, devotional accessed 8/9/2009.

WEEK 31: LIFT THE VEIL

23. Jack W. Hayford, ed., *Spirit Filled Life Bible* (Nashville: Thomas Nelson, 1991), 1795.

WEEK 41: THE POWER OF THE WIND

24. Martin Luther King Jr., "I've Been to the Mountaintop" speech, given April 3, 1968, to striking sanitation workers at Mason Temple, Memphis, TN. The entire text of this speech is available at http://americanrhetoric.com/speeches/mlkivebeentothemountaintop.htm.

WEEK 44: GOTTA GET YOUR SERVE ON

25. Both quotations from the Greenleaf Center for Servant Leadership, "What Is Servant Leadership," http://www.greenleaf.org/whatissl/; originally from Robert K. Greenleaf, *The Servant As Leader* (Robert K. Greenleaf Center, 1982), and Greenleaf, *The Institution As Servant* (Center for Applied Studies, 1972).

WEEK 48: EXPAND YOUR TERRITORY

26. Bruce H. Wilkinson, *The Prayer of Jabez* (Portland, OR: Multnomah Publishers, 2000).

27. Martin Luther King Jr., from "What Is Your Life's Blueprint?" a speech given to a group of students at Barratt Junior High School in Philadelphia on October 26, 1967, as reported in *The Seattle Times,* http://seattletimes.com/special/mlk/king/words/blueprint.html.

WEEK 49: THIS LITTLE LIGHT OF MINE, I'M GONNA LET IT SHINE!

28. Marianne Williamson, *A Return to Love: Reflections on the Principles of a Course in Miracles* (New York: HarperCollins, 1992), 164–5.

WEEK 52: I'M COMING OUT

29. Bernard Edwards and Nile Rodgers (1980), "I'm Coming Out," sung by Diana Ross on *Diana,* Motown, 1980, lyrics at http://www.metrolyrics.com/im-coming-out-lyrics-diana-ross.html. ©1980 Bernard's Other Songs and Sony Songs, Inc.